Abid Mahmood has been a barrister since 1992. He is recognised in law directories as a leading practitioner in four practice areas across England and Wales.

He has been sitting as a Judge in various jurisdictions since 2006, including at the Crown Court, County Court (civil law and family law) and at the Upper Tribunal and First-tier Tribunal (Immigration and Asylum Chamber).

As a barrister, he has appeared at all levels of cases, including in successful appeals as lead counsel at the Supreme Court.

Contempt of Court and the New Rules

Contempt of Court and the New Rules

Abid Mahmood
Barrister, Inner Temple
No.5 Barristers' Chambers

Law Brief Publishing

The information in this book was believed to be correct at the time of writing. All content is for information purposes only and is not intended as legal advice. No liability is accepted by either the publisher or author for any errors or omissions (whether negligent or not) that it may contain. Professional advice should always be obtained before applying any information to particular circumstances.

Published 2021 by Law Brief Publishing, an imprint of Law Brief Publishing Ltd
30 The Parks
Minehead
Somerset
TA24 8BT

www.lawbriefpublishing.com

Paperback: 978-1-912687-94-7

To Ammah & Abbah

and to

Nazmun Ismail, H, Y and M.

PREFACE

Contempt of Court remains a powerful tool to enable courts and tribunals to ensure that orders are complied with and that parties will conduct themselves appropriately.

High-profile contempt cases have again been reported across the media recently and that will continue, but there are also thousands of cases of injunctions considered daily by the courts with many leading to contempt applications thereafter. The new extended statement of truth will also mean that there will be many more contempt applications.

The Civil Procedure Rules and the Family Procedure Rules now provide for a much-welcomed streamlined procedure for contempt applications.

The previous case law remains, but in the past there were far too many cases in which the parties' failure to comply with procedure led to applications being dismissed or there having to be appeals because the court was not made aware of the correct procedure.

The courts' powers in contempt applications are significant. It is essential that the court continues to use that power correctly. Therefore, it is equally essential that the parties remind the court of the correct procedure and law.

The issue of legal representation and legal aid still remains confusing for many. In my view it is vital that claimants and the court make alleged contemnors (defendants) aware of their eligibility to non-means tested legal aid. At chapter four I have set out where and how that application for non-means tested legal aid can be made. I have also set out the contact details for the Legal Aid Agency.

This book will be of use to the judiciary, to practitioners, to corporate bodies and to litigants in person. I have provided a checklist at the end of the book for use as an aide-memoire and as a starting point and helpful guide.

I hope that armed with this book, readers will have resources available to them for use across a wide range of courts and tribunals. That includes at the High Court, Family Court, Court of Protection, Business and Property Court and Tribunals.

Readers who have suggestions or spot errors or omissions are warmly encouraged to write to me at No5 Barristers' Chambers.

The law is stated as at 1 July 2021.

Abid Mahmood
July 2021

CONTENTS

CHAPTER ONE

INTRODUCTION

Arlidge, Eady and Smith explains that from earliest legal history the courts have assumed power to coerce those who obstruct the administration of justice. The history of contempt is dealt with in a fascinating way, including with references to the Star Chamber and its possible influence on the common law.

In this book, I shall deal with the more recent attempts by the courts to 'coerce and persuade' persons and entities to comply with its orders and procedure.

What is Contempt?

The Report of the Committee on Contempt of Court, Command 5794 (1974) (The Phillimore Committee) said that,

> *"The law relating to contempt of court has developed over the centuries as a means whereby the courts may act to prevent or punish conduct which tends to obstruct, prejudice or abuse the administration of justice either in relation to a particular case or generally"*

Therefore, contempt of court deals with a variety of conduct which undermines or which may potentially undermine the course of justice. The law in respect of it is very detailed. Historically, the procedure has been difficult and inconsistent.

There are many different courts and tribunals and so there are varying references to contempt of court. I shall concentrate mainly on 'civil contempt' and disobedience of court orders, but I shall also deal briefly with criminal contempt and with the more well-known contempt 'in the face of the court'.

The law of contempt of court is a complex mix of relatively inconsistent common law cases, alongside statute. Added to the complexity is that the High Court and County Court have different jurisdictions.

The case law deals with liability, jurisdiction, procedure, evidence and sanctions. The power to make an order of committal to prison for up to two years, thereby affecting the liberty of the person means that contempt will continue to be of much interest by the public and lawyers alike.

As I shall explain below, the procedure for dealing with contempt since October 2020 is now more streamlined with the introduction of new Procedure Rules. Therefore, it is important to ensure that one is using the latest guidance and procedure.

Contempt being quasi-criminal proceedings has important duties placed on the claimant as 'quasi-prosecutor'. The liberty of the Defendant is at stake and so any serious procedural defects will usually be fatal to the contempt application.

CHAPTER TWO

CONTEMPT BY INDIVIDUALS AND BODY CORPORATES

Contempt applies to individuals but also to corporate bodies.

There is no doubt that there can be contempt proceedings against corporate bodies. Procedure and case law make that clear. Although it is obvious that a company is not a physical person, the sanctions against the company can be severe. The sanctions against the directors of the corporate body can include imprisonment.

In Director General of Fair Trading v Pioneer Concrete UK Ltd and others [1995] 1 A.C. 456 Lord Templeman made clear in the House of Lords when the Court of Appeal was overruled that (emphasis has been added),

> *"The decisions of the Court of Appeal in Smiths' case and in the instant case infringe two principles. The first principle is that a company is an entity separate from its members but, not being a physical person is only capable of acting by its agents. The second principle is that a company, in its capacity as supplier of goods, like any other person in the capacity of taxpayer, landlord or in any other capacity, falls to be judged by its actions and not by its language. An employee who acts for the company within the scope of his employment is the company. Directors may give instructions, top management may exhort, middle management may question and workers may listen attentively.* ***But if a worker makes a defective product or a lower manager accepts or rejects an order, he is the company."***

In addition, the court has wide powers to deal with the corporate body's contempt of court directly via a writ of sequestration if that corporate body has failed to comply with or if it has breached a court order.

A writ of sequestration is the way in which the court can order the seizure of the assets of the corporate body and retain them until there has been compliance with orders of the court.

I set out in chapter eight below Part 81 of the Civil Procedure Rules which was introduced in October 2020, but in summary, writs of sequestration remain an available option under CPR Part 81.

In Dar Al Arkan Real Estate Development Co and another v Refai and others [2014] EWCA Civ 715, [2015] 1 W.L.R. 135, Beatson LJ held that committal proceedings can have extra-territorial effect and thereby be applied to foreign directors (in this case Saudi Arabia). Beatson LJ also dealt with the duties of directors in respect of committal proceedings. He said,

> *"33. It was because, absent a power over the directors and officers of companies which disobey orders of the court, the court's disciplinary powers over them would be significantly weakened, that a policy decision was taken to, in the words of Arlidge, Eady & Smith on Contempt , 4th ed (2011), para 12-116, "exert pressure" on those who have accepted responsibility by virtue of their offices in the company. For a director or officer to be liable, it is necessary to show that he or she knew of and was responsible for the company's breach of the court order, undertaking to the court, or other contempt..."*

In my view, it is clear that directors cannot merely hide behind the corporate veil. The consequences of breaches of injunctions or court orders by corporate bodies can have very serious consequences for the directors. That will enable the court to use it full suite of powers. That therefore includes imprisonment of those directors under an order of committal.

In view of the very serious sanctions which can flow, any director of a corporate body should give careful and anxious scrutiny to court orders with penal notices and should ensure that any committal application is promptly and correctly dealt with.

When referring to the parties in contempt cases, I shall use the terms from the new CPR Part 81. Those being 'Claimant' and 'Defendant' in place of 'Applicant' and "Respondent'. In addition, I shall also use the term 'alleged contemnor' when referring to the person against whom the actual or proposed contempt of court proceedings relate.

CHAPTER THREE

THE DIFFERENT TYPES OF CONTEMPT

Lord Mansfield CJ said in *Morgan v Jones* (1773) Lofft 160, 176

> *"Most of the disputes in the world arise from words."*

Not unlike medicine or dentistry, the legal profession and the courts have had their own way of excluding laypeople from understanding the words they use in court or in documents. The law in England Law has grown up with the use of different languages including English, French and Latin. All of which were used interchangeably in our courts for centuries. In more recent times, since Lord Woolf's pronouncements as Master of the Rolls we use much less Latin in court and in legal documents, but even now some language and words remain obscure to many.

In this way, contempt of court is 'chameleon' or 'protean'. Although attempted many times, the courts and jurists have struggled to easily classify the varying types of contempt of court. Therefore, I seek to attempt to assist the reader with some of the more recent views of the senior courts.

There is much that can be said about the difference between criminal and civil contempt, but a lengthy history is not necessary in view of the helpful judgment of Lord Toulson in the Supreme Court's judgment in **Regina v O'Brien** [2014] UKSC 23, [2014] 1 A.C. 1246 when he succinctly explained,

> *37. There is a distinction long recognised in English law between "civil contempt", ie conduct which is not in itself a crime but which is punishable by the court in order to ensure that its orders are observed, and "criminal contempt". Among modern authorities, the distinction was explained in general terms in* ***Home Office v Harman*** *[1983] 1* ***AC 280*** *(in particular by Lord Scarman, at p 310)...*

> *38. Breach of an order made (or undertaking obtained) in the course of legal proceedings may result in punishment of the person against whom the order was made (or from whom the undertaking was obtained) as a form of contempt... However, a contempt of that kind does not constitute a criminal offence. Although the penalty contains a punitive element, its primary purpose is to make the order of the court effective. A person who commits this type of contempt does not acquire a criminal record.*
>
> *39. A criminal contempt is conduct which goes beyond mere non-compliance with a court order or undertaking and involves a serious interference with the administration of justice. Examples include physically interfering with the course of a trial, threatening witnesses or publishing material likely to prejudice a fair trial...*
>
> *42... It is necessary to look at the nature and purpose of the order. It is fallacious to argue that because the order was made by a criminal court, rather than a civil court, disobedience to the order amounts to a crime, whereas it would not have been a crime to disobey a similar order imposed by a civil court. The question whether a contempt is a criminal contempt does not depend on the nature of the court to which the contempt was displayed; it depends on nature of the conduct. To burst into a court room and disrupt a civil trial would be a criminal contempt just as much as if the court had been conducting a criminal trial. Conversely, disobedience to a procedural order of a court is not in itself a crime, just because the order was made in the course of criminal proceedings. To hold that a breach of a procedural order made in a criminal court is itself a crime would be to introduce an unjustified and anomalous extension of the criminal law. "Civil contempt" is not confined to contempt of a civil court. It simply denotes a contempt which is not itself a crime."*

Open Justice is vital, but reports in publications and the media can interfere with justice in ongoing criminal trials. The Contempt of Court Act 1981 is the main legislation in respect of proceedings for contempt if such reporting may have an impact on the course of criminal proceedings.

Further sub-divisions of contempt

Again, because of the historical way that the case law has built upon and because of different statutes over a long period of time, the categories of contempt do not fall into neat categories, and indeed they can overlap. I deal here with some of the more common situations which arise.

1. Contempt in the 'face of the court'.

There is frequently reference to 'contempt in the face of the court', but what does it actually mean?

It is the power to deal 'at once[1] with those who interfere with the administration of justice'. Therefore, it is a 'summary' process, albeit my view is that this is no longer appropriate 'to deal at once' with final decisions on contempt. There must be significant safeguards to this summary process, including the right to legal representation and to the right to silence. It means therefore that the days of imprisonment with an order for committal on the same morning following an outburst from a court attendee should not occur.

I will deal below at chapter eight with the procedure to be followed and at chapter nine with the penalties or sanctions which can be imposed for contempt in the face of the court, but the starting and end is that set out by the Court of Appeal in **Morris v Crown Office** [1970] 2 Q.B. 114

The celebrated Lord Denning M.R. set out the facts of **Morris,**

> *"A group of students, young men and young women, invaded the court. It was clearly prearranged. They had come all the way from their University of Aberystwyth. They strode into the well of the court. They flocked into the public gallery. They shouted slogans. They scattered pamphlets. They sang songs. They broke up the hearing. The judge had to adjourn. They were removed. Order was restored."*

Lord Denning went on to hold,

> *"…a judge of the High Court still has power at common law to commit instantly to prison for criminal contempt, and this power is not affected in the least by the provisions of the Act of 1967. The powers at common law remain intact. It is a power to fine or imprison, to give an immediate sentence or to postpone it, to commit to prison pending his consideration of the sentence, to bind over to be of good behaviour and keep the peace, and to bind over to come up for judgment if called upon. These powers enable the judge to give what is, in effect, a suspended sentence."*

At the time this must have been seen as a very harsh decision when the students in question were protesting about something as important as the protection and use of the Welsh language. Leading counsel for the students had submitted to the Court of Appeal that these were students of impeccable character from 'good and hard-working Welsh families'.

The students' downfall though was the disruption that they had caused to the proceedings. The issue was not the strength of their cause. To look at this another way, the courts do not prevent properly presented written and oral submissions, even if those submissions might be controversial. What the courts do not permit though, even if based on good intention, is a rally or demonstration within the court room itself.

In cases I have presented at the Royal Courts of Justice, the clients' cause was 'presented' outside the famous entrance on the Strand with supporters having placed banners on the railings, with placards or by supporters blowing whistles and shouting chants demanding justice. Such demonstrations with permission and agreement are permissible, but a repeat of such behaviour inside the court is not. The court will usually permit such interested parties in the case to remain in the court room's public gallery for as long as they wish, but the demonstrators must remain as mere observers and not vocal protesters or by holding up placards or the like. Courts and judges acknowledge that feelings and emotions will be running high in cases that come to them for consideration. ThejJudge though has to deal with the case efficiently and without disruption.

Any person attending court must therefore appreciate that the court has very wide powers indeed to ensure that they behave and act appropriately. The courts jealously guard the need to ensure that the sanctity of the court is upheld.

The judges in those cases remind the public gallery that they are free to remain but that the judge will make a decision on the evidence and submissions that are heard and not on how loud the protest might be. That has to be right. Sometimes those with the quietest voice or even no voice are the ones who need justice and the courts' assistance the most.

If the **Morris** protestors had caused serious disruption now, then since 1 October 2020 the procedure to deal with it is much more streamlined than it was previously.

That is because of the introduction of Civil Procedure Rules Part 81.6(1)[2]. That specifically refers to contempt in the face of the court and states,

> *81.6.— Cases where no application is made*
>
> *(1) If the court considers that a contempt of court (including a contempt in the face of the court) may have been committed, the court on its own initiative shall consider whether to proceed against the defendant in contempt proceedings.*
>
> *(2) Where the court does so, any other party in the proceedings may be required by the court to give such assistance to the court as is proportionate and reasonable, having regard to the resources available to that party.*
>
> *(3) If the court proceeds of its own initiative, it shall issue a summons to the defendant which includes the matters set out in rule 81.4(2)(a)-(s) (in so far as applicable) and requires the defendant to attend court for directions to be given.*
>
> *(4) A summons issued under this rule shall be served on the defendant personally and on any other party, unless the court directs otherwise. If rule 81.5(2) applies, the procedure there set out shall be followed unless the court directs otherwise.*

[2] The new CPR Part 81 in force from 1 October 2020

Therefore, the judge would now be able to deal with the protestors more efficiently as set out in this new provision.

Examples of contempt in the face of the court can include:

- Assaulting or threatening people in the court
- Assaulting or threatening the judge. Unfortunately, in recent times, the willingness of litigants to attack judges has become more commonplace and is to be deplored[3].
- Insulting the court
- Disrupting court proceedings
- Disrespectful or other bad behaviour in court
- Taking photographs in court/making recordings of proceedings

2. Contempt arising from the interference with due administration of justice and false statement of truth

Much of the case law deals with cases which are outside of the above 'contempt in the face of the court' category. A myriad of activities is capable of amounting to contempt which constitutes interference with the due administration of justice or with the interference with the course of justice in proceedings.

An example to explain this sub-division include a case in which a lawyer allegedly told his client to lie to the court about the extent of his injuries in a personal injury claim, thereby the lawyer was alleged to be interfering with the course of justice.

Another example relates to the intentional publication of Children Act 1989 proceedings when it was known that such publication was not permitted. Publication and reporting have become more important in

[3] See the recent decision of Mr Justice Cohen in **Durrell v Scaife** (February 2021) in which he made a committal order of imprisonment against a contemnor who had frightened a judge in court by his behaviour and for swearing at the judge.

recent times because of social media and blogging and because of a healthy interest by non-lawyers in the work and publication of court decisions. Many argue that there should be 'open justice' so that the work and decisions of, for example, the Family Court and Court of Protection ought to be more accessible. Since the pandemic and lockdown in March 2020 there have been many hearings observed by the public remotely but with sufficient safeguards put in place by the court to ensure that the non-party observers comply with confidentiality.

A recent example of the court needing to use old processes and lawyers use of them comes from the use of draft judgments. The higher courts frequently send out draft judgments to the parties for corrections to be made before that judgment is finalised and 'handed down'. The 'handing down' of the judgment is completed by the Judge providing copies of their written judgment at a set time and date in open court.

Until the handing down of the judgment, the draft judgments are referred to as embargoed judgments. This system is a tried and tested formula whereby the Judge's clerk communicates directly with the barrister's clerk. The Judge's clerk makes clear that the draft judgment is for the use of the barristers only and for the barrister to deal with any corrections to the draft judgment.

There are some historic examples of breaches when embargoed judgments have been published or used, but recently the Supreme Court in **Her Majesty's Attorney General v Crosland** [2021] UKSC 15 had the opportunity to consider this issue in some detail.

In **R (Friends of the Earth Ltd) v Heathrow Airport Ltd** [2020] UKSC 52; [2021] PTSR 190, the Supreme Court had heard an appeal in respect a proposed new runway at Heathrow Airport. An embargoed draft judgment had been sent out to the barristers and solicitors. Mr Timothy Crosland was an unregistered barrister who had represented one of the parties. His client was called Plan B Earth.

The Supreme Court referred in its judgment to the well-used process of draft embargoed judgments being sent out to the parties and the warnings written on such drafts and on communications from the court office to the parties. The Supreme Court said,

> *"7. The email from the judgments clerk sent with the draft judgment invited corrections to the draft judgment. It continued:*
>
> *"The judgment is strictly confidential until given. The contents of these documents are not for publication, broadcast or use on club tapes before judgment has been promulgated. The documents are issued in advance by the Justices of the Supreme Court on the understanding that no approach is made to any organisation or person about their contents before judgment is given (see paragraph 6.8.3 to 6.8.5 of Practice Direction 6)."*
>
> *8. The Practice Direction states in relevant part:*
>
>> *"6.8.3 The judgment of the Court is made available to certain persons before judgment is given. When, for example, judgment is given on a Wednesday morning, it is made available to counsel from 10.30 am on the previous Thursday morning. In releasing the judgment, the Court gives permission for the contents to be disclosed to counsel, solicitors (including solicitors outside London who have appointed London agents) and in-house legal advisers in a client company, Government department or other body. The contents of the judgment and the result of the appeal may be disclosed to the client parties themselves 24 hours before the judgment is to be given unless the Court or the Registrar directs otherwise. A direction will be given where there is reason to suppose that disclosure to the parties would not be in the public interest.*
>>
>> *6.8.4 It is the duty of counsel to check the judgment for typographical errors and minor inaccuracies. In the case of apparent error or ambiguity in the judgment, counsel are requested to inform the Judicial Support section as soon as possible. This should be done by email to Judicial Support no later than two working days before the date judgment is to be given. The purpose of disclosing the judgment is not to allow counsel to re-argue the case, and attention is drawn to the opinions of Lord Hoffmann and Lord Hope in R*

> *(Edwards) v Environment Agency [2008] UKHL 22; [2008] 1 WLR 1587.*
>
> *6.8.5 Accredited members of the media may on occasion also be given a printed copy of the judgment in advance by the Court's communications team. The contents of this document are subject to a strict embargo and are not for publication, broadcast or use on club tapes before judgment has been delivered. The documents are issued in advance solely at the Court's discretion, and in order to inform later reporting, on the strict understanding that no approach is made to any person or organisation about their contents before judgment is given."'*

The Supreme Court held that there had been a contempt of court by Mr Crosland and it said that Mr Crosland had interfered with the administration of justice.

In my view, Mr Crosland had 'protested' very much like the students from Aberystwyth University in **Morris**. The problem being that even if Mr Crosland's protest was for 'good reasons', the directions in the embargoed judgment and in the e-mails from the Supreme Court had to be complied with. Those directions were clear. The Supreme Court said,

> *"23. In the words of Lord Toulson in* ***Director of the Serious Fraud Office v O'Brien*** *[2014] UKSC 23; [2014] AC 1246, para 39: "A criminal contempt is conduct which goes beyond mere non-compliance with a court order or undertaking and involves a serious interference with the administration of justice". The present case is not a case involving a breach of an order by a party to litigation where the order has been made at the instance of an opposing party and its purpose is simply to protect the private rights of that other party. Rather the order was made in order to protect the administration of justice and its breach involves a general interference from which the administration of justice must be safeguarded; see, for example,* ***Attorney General v Yaxley-Lennon*** *[2019] EWHC 1791 (QB); [2020] 3 All ER 477, para 54;* ***Attorney General v Dallas*** *[2012] EWHC 156 (Admin); [2012] 1 WLR 991;* ***Solicitor General v Cox (Contempt of Court: Illegal Photography)*** *[2016] EWHC 1241 (QB); [2016] 2 Cr App*

R 15, para 73. Furthermore, the requirement of confidentiality was imposed directly by the court on the respondent, who was a representative of a party to the litigation. The strictly confidential basis upon which draft judgments are provided to parties is well established, as are the reasons underpinning the duty of confidentiality in this context; see, for example, ***Director of Public Prosecutions v P (No 2)*** *[2007] EWHC 1144 (Admin); [2008] 1 WLR 1024, paras 2 and 10 per Smith LJ;* ***R v Noshad Hussein*** *[2013] EWCA Crim 990, paras 1 to 2 per Treacy LJ. The potential damage to the administration of justice which breaches of this duty of confidentiality may cause has also been emphasised; see, for example,* ***P (No 2)*** *at para 10 per Smith LJ. A critical point here is that the respondent has interfered with the court's control of its own proceedings. We accept the submission on behalf of the Attorney General that the publication of the outcome of the appeal in breach of the embargo was an interference with the proper administration of justice.*

24. Moreover, we accept the submission on behalf the Attorney General that the threshold of seriousness is passed in this case. First, it is vital for the authority of the court and in the interests of legal certainty that its judgments should be delivered at a time of its choosing and in a definitive form. Published judgments must be accurate, complete and in final form. Leaks of draft judgments could undermine the authority of the court and its judgments."

Having found the contempt proved, the Supreme Court proceeded to deal with penalties for the contempt against the contemnor. Mr Crosland was ordered to pay a £5000 fine for his contempt of court. The Supreme Court said,

"50. Any penalty imposed must be necessary for the legitimate objective of maintaining the authority and impartiality of the judiciary and must be proportionate for that purpose. As a result, we have had regard to the extent of the interference with article 10 rights and the likely deterrent effect on the future exercise of article 10 rights. The sentence we propose to impose is, in our view, a necessary and proportionate penalty for the purpose of maintaining the authority of the judiciary and its judgments.

51. We also take into account that the respondent is of positive good character.

1. *In these circumstances, we propose to deal with this matter by the imposition of a fine. In coming to a conclusion as to the appropriate level of fine, we have taken account of the fact that the respondent faces disciplinary proceedings before his professional body. We have also taken account of what the respondent has told us about his income. We therefore impose a fine of £5,000. That fine will be enforceable in like manner to a judgment of the High Court for the payment of money under section 16(1)(a) of the Contempt of Court Act 1981."*

(3) Statements of Truth (CPR Part 22)/False statements (CPR Parts 31.23 and 32.14)

CPR Part 22 refers to those documents that must be verified by a statement of truth.

A Practice Direction supplements CPR Part 22. It brought in a new extended version of the statement of truth from 6 April 2020 and it has significantly increased the need for statements of case and witness statements to be read and considered very carefully before they are signed.

The new extended wording to be used in statements of truth must now also refer specifically that the signatory agrees that they understand they will be at risk of contempt of court if they have signed a document which has a false statement and if they signed the document without an honest belief of the contents.

As I set out below, the Practice Direction requires the statement of truth to be translated into the language used by the person signing it.

If the statement of truth is not signed or if it has been signed incorrectly, then the court has the option to dismiss that party's case or to refuse to admit the evidence. Therefore, the sanctions for failure to provide the correctly signed statement of truth are severe.

It is worth reflecting on why the statement of truth is so important. At the time of the introduction of the Civil Procedure Rules over 30 years ago in 1988 the new 'buzz words' were to deal with cases justly, fairly and proportionately. Parties were encouraged to come to a resolution if they were able to and without the need for the court having to make decision. Alternative Dispute Resolution was also encouraged. Witness statements were to set out the party's case and would stand as their evidence-in-chief, thereby preventing a long oral recital of that witness's evidence. It was much easier and quicker to read the witness statement than to have hours or even days of oral evidence from the witness as evidence-in-chief. That was all to be welcomed.

The thinking was that armed with the Claimant's witness evidence and with the Claimant's statement of case/pleadings, signed with statements of truth, the Defendants would then be able to take a good hard look at the strength of the Claimant's case. The idea being that because the evidence and pleadings had confirmed in the statement of truth that the Claimant's was all true, then it would enable the Defendant to consider whether it had a sufficient defence. The Defendant would could therefore consider suggesting a compromise or even to agree to the claim and submit to judgment.

Other provisions of the new CPR, such as Part 36 enabled without prejudice offers to be made, but with serious costs sanctions and interest to be paid if the Defendant failed to accept an offer and if that offer was beaten at trial. Therefore, this further encouraged the parties to think carefully about whether or not to proceed to trial.

In my view, the inadvertent serious side effect of the CPR was that costs increased significantly, even for relatively routine and straightforward road traffic claims with relatively minor whiplash-type injuries[4].

[4] The system for dealing with whiplash claim has recently been changed by the introduction of the 'Whiplash Reforms" on 31 May 2021. This states that there is now provision for a digital portal to make any claim for personal injuries valued at under £5,000. The claimant can settle their own claim without the use of a lawyer if they wish. The small claims limit for road traffic accident-related personal injury claims has increased from £1,000 to £5,000. In the small claims track, costs are not

The Defendants and insurers in such claims had a stark choice to make. Should the claim be defended with the risk that if the defence fails then tens of thousands of pounds will have to be paid in costs, despite the damages claimed being modest at around just one thousand pounds?

I am sure that insurance companies and their legal advisers will have settled claims despite suspicion and concerns about the claim. More so, they will have been influenced by the signed statement of truth from the Claimant's side. That would probably have nudged the insurers to settle more readily than they did before the introduction of the CPR. Indeed, in some cases, the 'penalty' interest and costs arising from CPR Part 36 would have taken away any hesitation that the insurers might have had about settling the claim.

The problem was that some of those signing statements of truth were not telling the truth. This led to it being easier for false claims to succeed. "All" that the Claimant needed to do was to sign a witness statement. The insurers for the Defendant would consider that signed witness statement but because whiplash injuries are very subjective and difficult to disprove, the insurers would more likely than not, make an offer of settlement.

The civil courts see many insurance companies and Defendants seeking to deal with what they say are fraudulent road traffic accident-related whiplash or credit hire claims. The case law on exaggerated or 'fundamental dishonesty" cases is extensive. The additional use of CPR Part 44 to make adverse costs orders in cases of exaggeration and fundamental dishonesty provides an extra reason for the parties to attempt to negotiate a settlement, rather than for the court to decide the issues.

The phenomena of exaggerated or fundamental dishonesty in road traffic accident- related claims will continue in this country as it does in other

usually recoverable. There is a new tariff of compensation for whiplash injuries setting out how much can be claimed for an injury.

countries but perhaps more now in the small claims jurisdiction of the county court rather than as fast track claims.

In my view, the extended statement of truth from 6 April 2020 introduces an important additional layer which will affect the culture of how these cases are dealt with. Indeed, the extended statement of truth will affect all cases which require a statement of truth.

The extended statement of truth makes clear to the author of the witness statement that they will be acting in contempt of court if they sign a false statement of truth. That is a powerful weapon available to the court, but also to the parties to ensure that what is said in the written statement is true and accurate.

I refer below to 'satellite litigation'. With the amended statement of truth, it is clear that there will be many more applications for permission to proceed with alleged contempt arising out falsely signed statements of truth. It would appear to me that the extended statement of truth encourages parties to bring to the court's attention those who have signed false statements of truth. I doubt this will be seen as satellite litigation if the person signing the statement of truth was attempting to seriously mislead the opposing party and the court.

The Practice Direction to CPR Part 22 clearly sets out the documents which need to be verified by a statement of truth and it sets out the form which the statement of truth must take, which is dependent upon the type of document being signed. The Practice Direction to CPR part 22 states as follows,

> *"Documents to be verified by a statement of truth*
>
> ***1.1*** *Rule 22.1(1) sets out the documents which must be verified by a statement of truth. The documents include:*
>
> *(1) a statement of case,*
>
> *(2) a response complying with an order under rule 18.1 to provide further information,*
>
> *(3) a witness statement,*

(4) an acknowledgment of service in a claim begun by the Part 8 procedure,

(5) a certificate stating the reasons for bringing a possession claim or a landlord and tenant claim in the High Court in accordance with rules 55.3(2) and 56.2(2),

(6) a certificate of service,

(7) a contempt application under Part 81.

***1.2** If an applicant wishes to rely on matters set out in his application notice as evidence, the application notice must be verified by a statement of truth*

***1.3** An expert's report should also be verified by a statement of truth. For the form of the statement of truth verifying an expert's report (which differs from that set out below) see Practice Direction 35.*

***1.4** In addition, the following documents must be verified by a statement of truth:*

(1) an application notice for –

(a) a third party debt order (rule 72.3),

(b) a hardship payment order (rule 72.7), or

(c) a charging order (rule 73.3);

(2) a notice of objections to an account being taken by the court, unless verified by an affidavit or witness statement;

(3) a schedule or counter-schedule of expenses and losses in a personal injury claim, and any amendments to such a schedule or counter-schedule, whether or not they are contained in a statement of case.

***1.5** The statement of truth may be contained in the document it verifies or it may be in a separate document served subsequently, in which case it must identify the document to which it relates*

1.6 Where the form to be used includes a jurat for the content to be verified by an affidavit then a statement of truth is not required in addition.

Form of the statement of truth

2.1 The form of the statement of truth verifying a statement of case, a response, an application notice, a certificate of reasons or a notice of objections should be as follows:

'[I believe][the (claimant or as may be) believes] that the facts stated in this [name document being verified] are true. I understand] [The (claimant or as may be) understands that proceedings for contempt of court may be brought against anyone who makes, or causes to be made, a false statement in a document verified by a statement of truth without an honest belief in its truth.'

2.2 The form of the statement of truth verifying a witness statement should be as follows (and provided in the language of the witness statement):

'I believe that the facts stated in this witness statement are true. I understand that proceedings for contempt of court may be brought against anyone who makes, or causes to be made, a false statement in a document verified by a statement of truth without an honest belief in its truth.'

2.2A The form of the statement of truth verifying a costs budget should be as follows:

'This budget is a fair and accurate statement of incurred and estimated costs which it would be reasonable and proportionate for my client to incur in this litigation.'

2.3 Where the statement of truth is contained in a separate document, the document containing the statement of truth must be headed with the title of the proceedings and the claim number. The document being verified should be identified in the statement of truth as follows:

(1) claim form: 'the claim form issued on [date]',

(2) particulars of claim: 'the particulars of claim issued on [date]',

(3) statement of case: 'the [defence or as may be] served on the [name of party] on [date]',

(4) application notice: 'the application notice issued on [date] for [set out the remedy sought]',

(5) witness statement: 'the witness statement filed on [date] or served on [party] on [date]'.

***2.4** The statement of truth verifying a witness statement must be in the witness's own language.*

***2.5** A statement of truth must be dated with the date on which it was signed."*

Whereas CPR Part 22 and the Practice Direction deals with statements of truth, I turn to CPR part 32.14 which deals with false statements. It states,

"CPR 32.14. False statements

Proceedings for contempt of court may be brought against a person who makes or causes to be made a false statement in a document, prepared in anticipation of or during proceedings and verified by a statement of truth, without an honest belief in its truth."

And CPR Part 31.23 states,

"False disclosure statements

(1) Proceedings for contempt of court may be brought against a person if he makes, or causes to be made, a false disclosure statement, without an honest belief in its truth."

Therefore, a party can seek permission to commence contempt of court proceedings when it is claimed that the alleged contemnor signed the statement of truth but had no honest belief in its truth and knew that it was likely to interfere with the course of justice. As I set out above and below, this is a powerful option open to litigants, but it is an option that the court insists must not be abused and must remain proportionate. The requirement to seek permission to bring such proceedings is an added filter available to the court to weed out less meritorious cases. The permission stage ensures that there is some judicial consideration of the proposed application before a substantive committal can proceed in these types of cases.

(4) Other examples of interference with the administration of justice.

> *"You remain under oath. Please do not discuss your evidence with anyone during the adjournment".*

That is a frequent direction given by judges at all courts and tribunals to witnesses who are in the middle of giving their evidence and when it is necessary to break, for example, for lunch or at the conclusion of that day's proceedings. What if the witness does speak with persons about his evidence, despite the judge's direction telling them not to?

In **Hughes Jarvis Ltd v Searle** [2019] EWCA Civ 1, [2019] 1 W.L.R. 2934 the Court of Appeal dealt with such an issue. Patten LJ said,

> *"35. There is no reported case in which a witness has been held to commit a contempt of this kind by discussing his evidence with a third party during an adjournment but the concept of interference with the administration of justice is a wide one and I would not exclude the possibility of a witness being held to be in contempt for discussing his evidence particularly if he or she did so with a view to providing the court with a recollection of events which the witness did not have or to providing false evidence. Whether what occurred amounted to a direct interference with the administration of justice would obviously depend on what was discussed, the reasons for it and the effect which it had on the trial process. In this case I am not persuaded that on the facts known to the judge there had been a criminal contempt of this kind.*
>
> *36. But in any event, the judge had no jurisdiction to deal with that species of contempt..."*

The Court of Appeal set out very clear guidance for judges dealing with alleged contempt in these sorts of proceedings. The Court of Appeal set out the errors at first instance and said, (emphasis has been added),

> *"57. When, as occasionally happens, an incident occurs during a trial which gives the trial judge cause for concern that the integrity of a*

witness's evidence might have been compromised, a measured approach is called for. ***The aim should almost always be to investigate the facts as far as necessary but otherwise to complete the trial with as little interruption as possible, leaving any question of whether there has been a contempt of court or whether any further action is warranted to be considered at the end of the proceedings after judgment has been given.*** *That was, regrettably, not the approach which the judge adopted in the present case.* ***The judge's response to Mr Jarvis's disclosure that he had spoken to somebody while the case was adjourned overnight about a matter touching his evidence could well serve as a case study in how not to deal with such a situation. As set out by Patten LJ, the judge found that Mr Jarvis was in contempt of court without following a fair procedure and first giving him a proper opportunity to explain himself. She then proceeded to make a committal order which she did not have jurisdiction to make and for which there was in any event no reasonable basis, once again without following a fair procedure. She also struck out HJL's claim and its defence to Mr Searle's counterclaim—a course of action which, for the reasons that Patten LJ has explained, was likewise unjustified.***

58. ***Most regrettable of all, in my view, was the judge's action in remanding Mr Jarvis in custody overnight before deciding whether to make a committal order.*** *The reasons which the judge gave for adopting this extraordinary course were contradictory. On the one hand, she said (in the passage quoted at para 18 above) that she was remanding him in custody because "I cannot trust Mr Jarvis not to effectively interfere with his own evidence by speaking to other people". But that explanation was obviously flawed. Even if there had been a reasonable basis for such mistrust—which in my view there was not—the risk was of the judge's own making: it was only because she did not allow Mr Jarvis to complete his evidence that any possibility of "interfering with his own evidence" arose. On the other hand, the judge also said (in the same passage) that "This is not about preventing further harm, this is about marking the seriousness of what has happened". This acknowledged that the purpose of the order was not preventative but punitive, but involved punishing Mr Jarvis by committing him to prison before hearing any evidence or submissions on whether a committal order was justified.* ***Furthermore, the very***

act of remanding him in custody overnight impaired his ability to give instructions or otherwise prepare for the committal hearing which the judge had peremptorily insisted should take place the next day.

59. Even if the judge had had jurisdiction to make a committal order, Mr Jarvis's conduct could on no reasonable and considered view have justified depriving him of his liberty for any length of time, let alone doing so in the circumstances and manner in which it was done in this case. ***Put shortly, the judge's action in remanding him overnight in custody was a misuse of judicial power.***

60. I agree with everything that Patten LJ has said and hope that, ***if any similar situation should occur in future, reference to his judgment will avoid any risk of repetition of any of the many errors made in the handling of this case."***

CHAPTER FOUR

LEGAL REPRESENTATION AND LEGAL AID

There is a right to legal representation and to legal aid.

In my view there have been far too many cases in the past in which alleged contemnors have appeared before a judge in contempt of court proceedings but where the alleged contemnor has remained without legal representation. It has meant that the alleged contemnor had not had the benefit of legal advice. Nor has that alleged contemnor been aware that legal aid is available. Unfortunately, in the past, the court has not always been aware of the availability of non-means-tested legal aid either.

In ***James v James*** [2018] EWCA Civ 1982, [2018] 8 WLUK 96 the Court of Appeal set aside an order for committal against an alleged contemnor made by a circuit judge in respect of failures to attend court and to provide a witness statement. It was a case considered before October 2020 and so it was dealing with the previous CPR Part 81. The Court of Appeal was provided with extensive detail in respect of the nature of the right to silence and for there to be legal representation, or for there to be at the very least for a proper opportunity to obtain legal representation. Many of the submissions I made were later incorporated within other judgments and within the new CPR Part 81, albeit some seemed a little too radical for the Court of Appeal at that time. Details were also provided to the Court of Appeal on how legal aid can be secured for such committal cases and even granted by the Court of Appeal itself and this was partly incorporated within the judgment.

In allowing the appeal Bean LJ, with whom David Richards LJ agreed said,

> *"Turning to the hearing of 11 July, the judge was clearly right to advise the appellant to obtain legal representation but it is unrealistic, in my view, to have supposed that she could successfully do this from prison*

> *in one-and-a-half days. The obligation under paragraph 15.6 of Practice Direction 81 appended to CPR Part 81 is an obligation on the court to have regard to the need for the contemnor to be made aware of the possible availability of criminal legal aid and how to contact the Legal Aid Agency, and to the need to give an unrepresented contemnor the opportunity to obtain legal advice."*

In **Haringey London Borough Council v Brown** [2017] at [46], McCombe LJ said:

> *"46. At least until some improvement is made to the drafting of the legislation...it seems to me that it is important that all involved in committal proceedings in the County Courts should be aware of the route to be taken in applying for legal aid in such proceedings. For my part, I would encourage the LAA, the Courts Service, the judiciary, the professions and the voluntary organisations (that assist litigants) to co-operate in ensuring at an early stage in committal proceedings that all concerned are aware of the authority to which legal aid applications in such cases are to be made and what the entitlements are. It may be that, as Mr Bridge submitted here, consideration should be given to the promulgation of standard directions on the subject, either on the application notice itself and/or in any preliminary order regulating the procedure in an individual case."*
>
> *I would echo that. It would surely not be rocket science for a court centre such as Central London County Court to have a standard handout to be given to contemnors in Ms James' position, not simply saying:* ***"You have a right to legal aid" but giving practical assistance about how and to whom an urgent application should be made."***

James v James does not appear to have been cited to the Court of Appeal in the subsequent case of **O (Committal: Legal Representation)** [2019] EWCA Civ 1721, [2019] 4 W.L.R. 140. Peter Jackson LJ when saying he would allow the appeal due to a lack of legal representation explained the background to the case and concluded as follows (emphasis has been added),

> 1. *On 2 October 2019, the appellant Adriana Ortega Zeifert was imprisoned for four weeks for disobedience of a High Court order.*

On 11 October we allowed her appeal and ordered her release. The appeal succeeded on the single procedural ground that the appellant, who ostensibly wished to be legally represented, was unrepresented at a hearing on 13 June at which a suspended committal was made and at a later hearing on 2 October when the suspension was lifted.

2. ***The case is a reminder that respondents to committal proceedings are entitled to be provided with legal representation if they want it and that they will qualify for non-means-tested legal aid. There is an obligation on the court to ensure that this protection is made available. Where this does not happen any resulting order for committal may be procedurally irregular.***

3. *PD37A of the Family Procedure Rules contains, in the same manner as CPR PD81, a list of matters to which the court must have regard at the hearing of a committal application. These include:*

   "12.5 The court will also have regard to the need for the respondent to be –

   (1) allowed a reasonable time for responding to the committal application including, if necessary, preparing a defence;

   (2) made aware of the possible availability of criminal legal aid and how to contact the Legal Aid Agency;

   (3) given the opportunity, if unrepresented, to obtain legal advice; and

   (4) if unable to understand English, allowed to make arrangements, seeking the assistance of the court if necessary, for an interpreter to attend the hearing."

In the interesting case of **All England Lawn Tennis Club (Championships) Ltd and others v McKay (Rev.1)** [2019] EWHC 2971 QB Chamberlain J dealt with the rather confusing way in which legal aid has to be sought and who is then to grant legal aid in contempt proceedings.

The case concerned a 'ticket tout' selling tickets for the Wimbledon Championships.

The nature of what frequently actually occurs in a judge's list is evident from this case. The alleged contemnor had not appeared before Chamberlain J. A short General Practitioner's medical note had been produced stating that the alleged contemnor was unwell. Chamberlain J explained that he been told that legal advice and representation had not yet secured. In these cases, the question can be simple: should the judge merely deal with the contempt and make a decision because it was inevitable that there was no 'defence' or should the judge allow the alleged contemnor time to obtain legal advice and legal representation? Just because the question can be simply put does not mean that the decision-making or answer is easy.

Chamberlain J identified the difficulties in following the legal aid regulations. He said, (emphasis has been added),

> *"24…However, the authorities I have mentioned indicate that* ***there is a serious lack of clarity about how to go about making an application for legal aid for representation in respect of a committal for breach of an order made in civil proceedings.***
>
> *25. The uncertainty arises in the following way. Section 16 of the Legal Aid, Sentencing and Punishment of Offenders Act 2012 provides that legal aid for the purposes of criminal proceedings is to be available to an individual if he is a 'specified individual' and 'the relevant authority' has determined that he qualifies for representation. There is no doubt that an individual facing proceedings for committal for breach of a civil order is a 'specified individual'. This is because, although only one type of contempt proceedings (contempt in the face of the court) is specified in s.14 of the 2012 Act, civil contempt proceedings are treated as criminal for the purpose of Article 6(3) of the ECHR and proceedings so treated are treated as criminal by reg. 9(v) of the Criminal Legal Aid (General) Regulations 2013 .*
>
> *26.* ***The real issue is not whether legal aid is available, but who has the power to grant it: the court or the Legal Aid Agency.*** *Regulation 7 of the Criminal Legal Aid (Determinations by a Court and Choice of Representative) Regulations 2013 governs*

determinations by the High Court. Looking at that regulation on its own, the reader might well conclude that the High Court's power to make a determination that a person is entitled to legal aid arises only in the cases there set out, which do not include contempt proceedings for breach of a civil order. However, in King's Lynn and West Norfolk BC v Bunning [2015] 1 WLR 531 , Blake J held – accepting submissions made to him on behalf of the LAA and having considered the statutory scheme in considerable detail – that reg. 7 does not preclude the High Court from making a determination in such a case. That decision was followed by Sir James Munby, President of the Family Division, in Chelmsford County Court v Ramet [2014] 2 FLR 1084 ; and it was at least assumed by the Court of Appeal to be correct in Brown .

27. In H v T (Committal Appeal: Notice on Orders) [2018] 4 WLR 122 , Baker J recorded submissions made to him by the Legal Aid Agency that Blake J's conclusion in Bunning (expressly accepting submissions made to him by Agency) was wrong; and it was the Agency, not the court, which had power to make legal aid determinations in contempt proceedings for breach of a civil order. He did not in the event have to determine that question. "

There were further hearings relating thereafter before Chamberlain J, but the same case was also heard by HHJ Freedman and Nicol J. Ultimately, the matter was to be considered by the Court of Appeal upon the appeal of Mr McKay[5].

At the Court of Appeal, Henderson LJ noted the second judgment of Chamberlain J at which he had seen written evidence from the Legal Aid Agency. Henderson LJ said,

"39. At the adjourned hearing on 8 November 2019, Mr McKay attended in person. The court heard submissions from Mr Rimer of the LAA, and proceeded to deal in substance with the question whether the court or the LAA was the appropriate body to grant funding in civil contempt applications, deciding that the LAA was: see [2019] EWHC

[5] **Luke McKay v The All England Law Tennis Club (Championships) Limited and another** [2020] EWCA Civ 695, [2020] 6 WLUK 1

> *3065 (QB). Mr Rimer informed the court that Mr McKay would be entitled to legal aid without any assessment of means or of the merits of the case, and that such applications were normally determined within 48 hours. Accordingly, once [the advocate for Mr Mckay] had met his client, he should make an application for criminal legal aid to be granted by sending an application to a designated email address."*

My experience is that it can now be reasonably straightforward to seek legal aid for committal proceedings. As I have explained above, it may well be that the proceedings are seen as <u>civil proceedings</u>. That may be so, but it is <u>criminal</u> legal aid that has to be sought. There is a specialist unit of the Legal Aid Agency in Nottingham that deals with Legal Aid for contempt proceedings. The cases I have been instructed on have covered a wide geographical area across England and Wales and across numerous areas of law. The Nottingham LAA unit dealt legal aid funding for them all.

For example, in **Mushtaq and others v Hashmat and others (2MA30052)**, His Honour Judge Pearce sitting as a Judge of the High Court at Manchester dealt with very lengthy contempt proceedings. These proceedings were compromised by way of a Tomlin Order after several days of evidence was heard from witnesses via video link from abroad in pre-Covid times. The original proceedings related to Business and Property Court matters and therefore not of a criminal nature at all. Indeed, it assisted that the solicitors acting for the alleged contemnors included AGI Criminal Solicitors. The expertise of criminal law solicitors in dealing with committal proceedings in which the criminal standard of proof applies can be useful and of importance.

<u>MAKING THE APPLICATION FOR LEGAL AID</u>

The Legal Aid Agency's website page explains how legal aid can be obtained. I refer to it in full.

> "Providers dealing with civil contempt cases can now apply for criminal legal aid to represent clients for committal proceedings.

Applications are made to the National Courts Team (NCT) in Nottingham. This is to allow clients to be represented in breach or contempt proceedings including the breach of a civil order.

Providers should not apply to the Legal Aid Agency (LAA) for an amendment to an existing civil certificate or submit a fresh civil legal aid application for this work. This is because it can only be funded under criminal legal aid.

It is important to note that in order to carry out committal work in civil contempt cases you must be authorised to both undertake criminal legal aid and apply for a representation order.

Why criminal legal aid?

Civil contempt proceedings are seen as criminal for the purposes of legal aid because of the risk of imprisonment for your client.

How the application process works

All applications for criminal legal aid in committal proceedings should be submitted to the NCT in Nottingham.

You need to use the paper CRM14 form and also include a copy of the committal application.

If you do not hold a crime contract then you should apply for an Individual Case Contract (ICC) by writing to the Nottingham NCT – see email address below.

Your email will need to explain why you are applying and how you meet the ICC criteria.

More detail on making an application is available in our guidance on applications in civil contempt cases – see below.

Applications under the previous arrangements

If you follow the previous arrangements your application is likely to be delayed. So you are strongly advised to use the CRM14 form for legal aid in contempt cases and submit this application to NCT.

Payment claims

All claims for payment should be submitted to the crime finance team in Nottingham using the CRM11 form – see below.

The applicable rates of remuneration are set out in the Criminal Legal Aid (Remuneration) Regulations 2013 – see below.

Consultation on civil contempt payments

The Ministry of Justice (MOJ) intends to carry out a policy consultation exercise later this year regarding remuneration arrangements in civil contempt cases both at the Family Court and more widely.

Further information

Nottingham.NCT@legalaid.gsi.gov.uk – to submit Individual case contract applications

Apply for legal aid for civil contempt cases – for guidance and CM11 form

CRM14: criminal legal aid application form – to download paper form

Criminal Legal Aid Remuneration Regulations"

Therefore, in the County Court, the family court and the High Court it is clear that the Legal Aid Agency will grant non means tested legal aid. The application to be made is for criminal legal aid.

There is some support for the contention that at the Court of Appeal the court can itself grant legal aid for contempt proceedings. See the Criminal

Legal Aid (General) Regulations 2013 at Regulation 4(2) and 8. There is no means-test if the Court of Appeal is to grant funding.

CHAPTER FIVE

GYPSY AND TRAVELLER CASES

In **London Borough Havering v Clarke and others** (QB 2020 003382, QB 2021 000094) the High Court has been dealing with allegations of breaches of without notice injunction orders by person in the traveller community. The genesis of that case being planning law, but again the contempt proceedings then led to the need to obtain a grant of criminal legal aid. That legal aid having been granted by the LAA unit in Nottingham.

Legal Aid is also available for in respect of issues relating to homes for Gypsies and Travellers to defend in planning injunctions or to make appeals and applications by virtue of section 288 and 289 of the Town and Country Planning Act.

The use of wide injunctions against 'persons unknown' has been the subject of recent consideration by Nicklin J in a detailed judgment in **London Borough of Barking and Dagenham and others v Persons Unknown and others** [2021] EWHC 1201 (QB). Nicklin J held,

> *233. Can the local authorities demonstrate that Traveller Injunctions fall into the exceptional category where the court is compelled to act by way of contra mundum injunction? In my judgment, the answer is plainly no. There is no doubt that Traveller Injunctions engage the Article 8 rights of Gypsies and Travellers: LB Bromley (see [15] above). Insofar as the remaining local authorities in the Cohort Claims, now raise an argument that the relief sought also engages the Article 8 rights of denizens of its area, then the Court would be required to perform the required parallel analysis when considering whether to grant an injunction and, if so, in what terms. The Court's task in doing so was explained by Sir Mark Potter P in A Local Authority v W [2006] 1 FLR 1 [53] :*
>
> *"... The exercise of parallel analysis requires the court to examine the justification for interfering with each right and the issue of*

> *proportionality is to be considered in respect of each. It is not a mechanical exercise to be decided upon the basis of rival generalities. An intense focus on the comparative importance of the specific rights being claimed in the individual case is necessary before the ultimate balancing test in terms of proportionality is carried out..."*

Some of the counsel in the case have confirmed to me that this issue of injunctions against persons unknown is now to be considered by the Court of Appeal. It will be interesting to see whether there can be such wide injunctions in the form contended for by local authorities or whether the restrictions continue to require evaluative consideration of proportionality and interference with the homes of the travellers or gypsies, including children.

In **Cheshire East Borough Council v Michael Moloney and others** [2021] EWHC 1156 (QB) Turner J dealt with the contempt and penalties of various persons of a traveller community who had breached injunction orders and planning matters. Turner J suspended an order of committal to prison and made an order for costs against the Defendants.

CHAPTER SIX

COURTS AND TRIBUNALS

Family Courts

Part 37 of the Family Procedure Rules 2010 mirror the Civil Procedure Rules Part 81 and were both introduced at the same time on 1 October 2020.

The courts are very used to dealing with a wide variety of cases in which it is alleged that litigants have failed to comply with orders. This is perhaps particularly acute in the family courts. The applications for what used to be called 'ouster orders' to remove persons from the family home were listed in family court lists on a daily basis. There were hundreds of such cases across the country each day. There are perhaps less cases now of this type since the introduction of Part IV of the Family Law Act 1996, and with more criminal law powers, but nonetheless there are very many applications and orders for non-molestation injunctions within family proceedings against partners and spouses seeking protection for the resident spouse/partner and/or children.

There is frequent use of undertakings in family courts. The advantage to the provider of the undertakings being that there they are making no admissions of the allegations raised against them in the application for an injunction. Instead, the person is making a promise to the court set out in the signed undertakings form (there are standard forms available in the court for such purposes). The provider of the undertakings promise that they will abide by the terms set out within that undertakings form. The advantage for the person applying for the injunction being that it saves time and cost not having to litigate the matter and it avoids the rather personal family issues having to be considered by the court. The advantage for the provider of the undertakings is that there are no actual findings made. There is also an advantage for busy courts too, because the other cases waiting to be heard and listed can then take this case's place.

The court must explain to the person providing the undertaking that if in the future it is alleged that the undertaking has been broken then the applicant can issue committal proceedings against them. The Court will also stress to the provider of the undertaking that they must abide by the undertakings and that if any breach of the undertaking is proved then the court can deal with that breach with serious sanctions, including with imprisonment by an order of committal for up to 2 years.

A retired judge, His Honour Judge Fletcher sitting at Wolverhampton in the late 1990's and early 2000's had a very clear way of communicating this to the person entering into undertakings. I vividly recall HHJ Fletcher. He left a very good impression on me when I was counsel in many cases before him. Sometimes I would be acting for the applicant and at other times for the respondent. These things might seem standard now because they are contained within the Equal Treatment Bench Book and in other places, but I recall the care and patience that HHJ Fletcher showed when he would look to the respondent and politely explain something like the following. This remains very useful for me when I now hear cases,

"Mr Smith, I want you to be clear that I have not made any findings of fact against you. I understand that you wish to enter into undertakings. You and I have a copy of the same document in front of us [HHJ Fletcher would then read out the undertakings form and ask "Mr Smith" to follow the document with him]. Mr Smith, I want you to know that all this undertaking is asking you to do is to allow Mrs Smith to go about her normal everyday business. As the undertaking states, you must not threaten, harass or pester Mrs Smith and you must not use violence against her. Nor must you instruct or encourage any other person to do so. Do you understand those things? I want you to be absolutely clear. I also want you to be absolutely clear that if you break the undertakings which are promises that you are making to the Court, then Mrs Smith may bring proceedings for contempt of court against you. That would be very serious because if the contempt is found to be proved then the Court will have to sentence you for contempt of court. The court's powers are very wide and can include a fine or a suspended sentence, but this Court and other Courts quite frequently decide that the breach of the promise to the court is so serious that a sentence of imprisonment will follow. The Court's maximum powers include a power to impose a sentence of imprisonment for up to two years. Therefore, please let me ask you again. Do you fully understand all of this? If you do then please sign the undertakings form on the back and I shall arrange for you to take a photocopy with you before you leave court today".

As can be seen, it is vital that the person entering the undertaking actually understands what (s)he is promising to do or not to do. Similarly, it is vital that the person against whom any injunction order is made understands what (s)he is being asked to do or to refrain from doing. To the lawyers it might seem like standard wording which they see and hear daily, but for a litigant, being in court is of itself a nerve wracking and unusual experience. Ensuring that the person understands the undertakings or injunction order is vital.

Also in the Family Court, there are numerous cases involving alleged breaches of 'contact' orders (Section 8 Children Act 1989 Child Arrangements Orders). In addition, there are relatively frequent Forced Marriage Protection Orders. Although they have a technicality about them, the contempt procedures can be used to assist to ensure that the necessary information about the person to be protected is obtained swiftly.

It is much more efficient to take the time to explain to the person entering the undertaking or against whom an injunction is made at the outset. That is because in the medium to long term they are then less likely to breach the undertakings or injunction order as they will more clearly know and fully understand what the consequences might be if they do breach the orders.

It will be recalled that although contempt proceedings have a punishment element to them, there is also the importance of seeking to 'persuade' or to 'coerce' the uncooperative party. Used imaginatively and correctly, contempt powers enable the court to make orders to successfully prevent harm to children and adults.

Civil Courts

The expertise of the civil courts with specialist courts and judges in England and Wales means that there will be a wide variety of case in which contempt proceedings can arise. Such contempt applications will include in commercial law in the Business and Property Court. It will also include Queen's Bench Division cases. There will also be alleged breaches in planning matters. Each application though has to comply with the same requirements to ensure that there is compliance with fundamental procedural fairness. The courts are adept at ensuring that is done, albeit contempt proceedings and procedure was previously very confusing with so many different approaches available in different courts and scenarios.

There are further sub-categories of the civil courts. The High Court is a superior court of record and the Chancery, Family and Queen's Bench Divisions will usually hear the contempt application. Such cases will be heard by a puisne judge (High Court Judge) or a person so authorised, but some contempt cases are still heard in the Divisional Court. At the Divisional Court there will frequently be a Lord/Lady Justice of Appeal who will sit with a puisne judge in Divisional Court business. The Administrative Court, perhaps more easily described as the specialist judicial review court, also hears case of substance and obviously also has the full range of powers when dealing with contempt applications.

The County Court gets its powers from s118 of the County Courts Act 1984. There is jurisdiction for both district judges and circuit judges to deal with contempt, including by deputy district judges and frequently by Recorders. Indeed, in some court centres across the country, it is the district judge bench which is the specialist bench as it deals daily with injunctions, be they Anti-Social Behaviour Order applications or family law injunctions. However, the County Court's jurisdiction to hear contempt cases is not as extensive as the High Court. See too CPR Part 81.3(2) which provides,

> *"81.3 (2) If the application is made in the High Court, it shall be determined by a High Court judge of the Division in which the case is proceeding. If it is made in the county court, it shall be determined by a Circuit Judge sitting in the county court, unless under a rule or practice direction it may be determined by a District Judge".*

<u>Court of Protection</u>

The Court of Protection makes welfare and financial decisions on behalf of persons who lack the mental capacity to do so. The current Court of

Protection was established by the Mental Capacity Act 2005. Section 45 makes clear it is a superior court of record.

With the number of deprivation of liberty cases and with regionalisation whereby the Court of Protection sits across England and Wales with 'nominated judges'[6] there have been thousands of cases each year.

The Court of Protection Rules 2017 has similar overriding objectives to those in the civil, family and criminal jurisdictions. Part 21 of the Rules deals with contempt applications.

There is also a Court of Protection Practice Direction which deals with contempt of court. It is worth setting it out in full.

> *"PRACTICE DIRECTION 21A – CONTEMPT OF COURT*
>
> *This practice direction supplements Part 21 of the Court of Protection Rules 2017*
>
> *Section 2 of Part 21 – Committal for breach of a judgment, order or undertaking to do or abstain from doing an act*
>
> *Requirement for a penal notice on judgments and orders – form of penal notice (Rule 21.9)*
>
> *1. A judgment or order which restrains a party from doing an act or requires an act to be done must, if disobedience is to be dealt with by proceedings for contempt of court, have a penal notice endorsed on it as follows (or in words to substantially the same effect)—*
>
> *"If you the within-named [ ] do not comply with this order you may be held to be in contempt of court and imprisoned or fined, or your assets may be seized."*
>
> *Requirement for a penal notice on judgments and orders – undertakings (Rule 21.9)*

[6] Tier 1 are District Judges, Tier 2 are Circuit Judges and Tier 3 are High Court Judges

2.1. Subject to rule 21.9(2) (which covers the case where the undertaking is contained in an order or judgment), the form of an undertaking to do or abstain from doing any act must be endorsed with a notice setting out the consequences of disobedience as follows (or in words to substantially the same effect)—

"You may be held to be in contempt of court and imprisoned or fined, or your assets may be seized, if you break the promises you have given to the court."

2.2. The court may decline to— (a) accept an undertaking; or

(b) deal with disobedience in respect of an undertaking by contempt of court proceedings.

unless the party giving the undertaking has made a signed statement to the effect that the party understands the terms of the undertaking and the consequences of failure to comply with it, as follows (or in words to substantially the same effect)—

"I understand the undertaking that I have given and that if I break any of my promises to the court I may be sent to prison, or fined, or my assets may be seized, for contempt of court."

2.3. The statement need not be made before the court in person. It may be endorsed on the court copy of the undertaking or may be filed in a separate document such as a letter.

Section 3 of Part 21 – Contempt in the face of the court

Committal for contempt in the face of the court (Rule 21.12)

3.1. Where the committal proceedings relate to a contempt in the face of the court the matters referred to in paragraph 3.3 should be given particular attention. Normally it will be appropriate to defer consideration of the respondent's actions and behaviour to allow the respondent time to reflect on what has occurred. The time needed for the following procedures should allow such a period of reflection.

3.2. The use of the Part 10 procedure is not required for contempt in the face of the court, but other provisions of this practice direction should be applied, as necessary, or adapted to the circumstances.

3.3. The judge should—

(a) tell the respondent of the possible penalty that the respondent faces;

(b) inform the respondent in detail, and preferably in writing, of the actions and behaviour of the respondent which have given rise to the committal application;

(c) if the judge considers that an apology would remove the need for the committal application, tell the respondent;

(d) have regard to the need for the respondent to be—

(i) allowed a reasonable time for responding to the committal application, including, if necessary, preparing a defence;

(ii) made aware of the possible availability of criminal legal aid and how to contact the Legal Aid Agency;

(iii) given the opportunity, if unrepresented, to obtain legal advice;

(iv) if unable to understand English, allowed to make arrangements, seeking the court's assistance if necessary, for an interpreter to attend the hearing; and

(v) brought back before the court for the committal application to be heard within a reasonable time;

(e) allow the respondent an opportunity to—

apologise to the court;

explain the respondent's actions and behaviour; and

if the contempt is proved, to address the court on the penalty to be imposed on the respondent; and

(f) where appropriate, nominate a suitable person to give the respondent the information. (It is likely to be appropriate to nominate a person where the effective communication of information by the judge to the respondent was not possible when the incident occurred.)

3.4. If there is a risk of the appearance of bias, the judge should ask another judge to hear the committal application.

3.5. Where the committal application is to be heard by another judge, a written statement by the judge before whom the actions and behaviour of the respondent which have given rise to the committal application took place may be admitted as evidence of those actions and behaviour.

Section 5 of Part 21 – Committal for making a false statement of truth

Committal application in relation to a false statement of truth (Rule 21.17)

4.1. Rule 21.17(1)(b) provides that a committal application may be made by the Attorney General. However the Attorney General prefers a request that comes from the court to one made direct by a party to the proceedings in which the alleged contempt occurred without prior consideration by the court. A request to the Attorney General is not a way of appealing against, or reviewing, the decision of the judge.

4.2. Where the permission of the court is sought under rule 21.17(1)(a), the affidavit evidence in support of the application must—

(a) identify the statement said to be false;

(b) explain—

(i) why it is false; and

(ii) why the maker knew the statement to be false at the time it was made; and

(c) explain why contempt proceedings would be appropriate in the light of the overriding objective in Part 1 of the Rules.

4.3. The court may—

(a) exercise any of its powers under the Rules (including the power to give directions under rule 21.15(6));

(b) initiate steps to consider if there is a contempt of court and, where there is, to punish it; or

(c) as provided by rule 21.17(3), direct that the matter be referred to the Attorney General with a request to consider whether to bring proceedings for contempt of court.

4.4. A request to the Attorney General to consider whether to bring proceedings for

contempt of court must be made in writing and sent to the Attorney General's Office at 5-8 The Sanctuary, London SW1P 3JS.

4.5. A request to the Attorney General must be accompanied by a copy of any order directing that the matter be referred to the Attorney General and must—

(a) identify the statement said to be false;

(b) explain—

(i) why it is false; and

(ii) why the maker knew the statement to be false at the time it was made; and

(c) explain why contempt proceedings would be appropriate in the light of the overriding objective in Part 1 of the Rules.

4.6. Once the applicant receives the result of the request to the Attorney General, the applicant must send a copy of it to the court that will deal with the committal application, and the court will give such directions as it sees fit.

4.7. The rules do not change the law of contempt or introduce new categories of contempt. A person applying to commence such proceedings should consider whether the incident complained of does amount to contempt of court and whether such proceedings would further the overriding objective in Part 1 of the Rules.

Section 6 of Part 21 – Writ of sequestration to enforce a judgment, order or undertaking

Requirement for a penal notice on judgments and orders (Rule 21.24)

5. Paragraphs 1 and 2.1 to 2.3 apply to judgments or orders to be enforced by a writ of sequestration (subject in the case of undertakings to rule 21.24(2), which covers the case where the undertaking is contained in an order or judgment).

Levying execution on certain days

6. Unless the court orders otherwise, a writ of sequestration to enforce a judgment, order or undertaking must not be executed on a Sunday, Good Friday or Christmas Day.

Section 7 of Part 21 – General rules about committal applications, orders for committal and writs of sequestration

Human rights

7. In all cases the Convention rights of those involved should particularly be borne in mind. It should be noted that the standard of proof, having regard to the possibility that a person may be sent to prison, is that allegation be proved beyond reasonable doubt.

(Section 1 of the Human Rights Act 1998 defines "the Convention rights".)

Applications for committal after permission granted or where permission not needed

8.1. An application for an order of committal must be commenced by filing a COP9 application notice in accordance with Part 21.

8.2. The applicant must file the original and one copy of the application notice, together with the original and one copy of the affidavit that is required by rule 21.10.

8.3. The affidavit must contain—

(a) the name and description of the person making the application;

(b) the name, address and description of the person sought to be committed;

(c) the grounds on which committal is sought;

(d) a description of each alleged act of contempt, identifying:

(i) each act separately and numerically, and

(ii) if known, the date of each act; and

(e) any additional information required by paragraphs 8.4 and 8.5.

8.4. Where the allegation of contempt relates to prior proceedings before the court, the affidavit must also state:

(a) the case number of those prior proceedings;

(b) the date of the proceedings; and

(c) the name of P.

8.5. The affidavit must also set out in full any order, judgment or undertaking which it is alleged has been disobeyed or broken by the person sought to be committed. This will apply where the allegation of contempt is made on the grounds that—

(a) a person is required by a judgment or order to do an act, and has refused or neglected to do it within the time fixed by the judgment or order or any subsequent order;

(b) a person has disobeyed a judgment or order requiring that person to abstain from doing an act; or

(c) a person has breached the terms of an undertaking which that person gave to the court.

(Practice Direction A accompanying Part 14 sets out further details in relation to affidavits.)

Evidence

9.1. Written evidence in support of or in opposition to a committal application must be given by affidavit.

9.2. Written evidence served in support of or in opposition to a committal application must, unless the court directs otherwise, be filed.

9.3. The following rules do not apply to committal applications—

(a) rule 15.12 (Court's power to direct that evidence is to be given by a single joint expert); and

(b) rule 15.13 (Instructions to single joint expert).

Hearing of application (Rule 21.28)

10.1. When filing the application notice, the applicant must obtain from the court a date for the hearing of the committal application.

10.2. Unless the court otherwise directs, the hearing date of a committal application must not be less than 14 days after service of the application notice on the respondent. The hearing date must be specified in the application notice or in a Notice of Hearing attached to and served with the application notice.

10.3. The court may at any time give case management directions (including directions for the service of evidence by the person sought to be committed and evidence in reply by the applicant) or may hold a directions hearing.

10.4. The court may on the hearing date—

(a) give case management directions with a view to a hearing of the committal application on a future date; or

(b) if the committal application is ready to be heard, proceed forthwith to hear it.

10.5. Where the person sought to be committed gives oral evidence at the hearing (in accordance with rule 21.28(2)), he or she may be cross-examined.

10.6. In dealing with any committal application, the court will have regard to the need for the respondent to have details of the alleged acts of contempt and the opportunity to respond to the committal application.

10.7. The court will also have regard to the need for the respondent to be—

(a) allowed a reasonable time for responding to the committal application including, if necessary, preparing a defence;

(b) made aware of the possible availability of criminal legal aid and how to contact the Legal Aid Agency;

(c) given the opportunity, if unrepresented, to obtain legal advice; and

(d) if unable to understand English, allowed to make arrangements, seeking the assistance of the court if necessary, for an interpreter to attend the hearing.

Striking out, procedural defects and discontinuance

11.1. On application by the respondent or on its own initiative, the court may strike out a committal application if it appears to the court—

(a) that the application and the evidence served in support of it disclose no reasonable ground for alleging that the respondent is guilty of a contempt of court;

(b) that the application is an abuse of the court's process or, if made in existing proceedings, is otherwise likely to obstruct the just disposal of those proceedings; or

(c) that there has been a failure to comply with a rule, practice direction or court order.

11.2. The court may waive any procedural defect in the commencement or conduct of a committal application if satisfied that no injustice has been caused to the respondent by the defect.

11.3. A committal application may not be discontinued without the permission of the court."

In <u>MASM v MMAM (by her litigation friend, the Official Solicitor), MM, London Borough of Hackney, Homerton University Hospital NHS Foundation Trust</u> [2015] 3 WLR 190

Hayden J explained that although contempt proceedings in the Court of Protection will be rare, a mechanism was in place to deal with such cases and to fend of problems before they get to the contempt stage. He said,

> *"53. Though this case raises important issues of law and practice it must be emphasised that conduct of the kind seen here is rare, indeed in my experience it is unprecedented. Many of the litigants who come before the Court of Protection are at a time of acute distress in their lives, as a cursory glance at the case law of this still fledgling court will show. The issues could not be more challenging, not infrequently they quite literally involve decisions relating to life and death. Inevitably, some litigants do not achieve their objectives neither wholly nor in part but they respect the process. More than once I have observed that the importance to a family of being heard in decisions of this magnitude matters almost as much as the outcome itself. Sometimes the medical and ethical issues raised are such that NHS trusts seek the authorisation of the court to endorse or reject a particular course of action. The court ultimately gives its conclusion by declaration both in relation to lawfulness and best interests. The terms of these declarations often cannot and indeed should not seek to be too prescriptive.*
>
> *54. Another category of case which frequently arises (as here) is where an elderly relative suffering from dementia requires specialist and residential care. Partners or relatives sometimes struggle to accept the privations that are often necessary in such circumstances and there occasionally can be conflict. Frequently, these issues resolve themselves but it would to my mind be disproportionate and indeed corrosive of the co-operation ultimately required, for the shadow of potential contempt proceedings to fall too darkly over cases such as this. It would not be an appropriate response to this judgment for the profession to over burden future orders too readily with penal notices. "*

<u>Crown Court</u>

As a superior court of record it has similar powers to that of the High Court pursuant to s45(4) Senior Courts Act 1981. Part 48 of the Criminal Procedure Rules 2015 set out the applicable rules for committal applications.

Tribunals

The Tribunals, Courts and Enforcements Act 2007 replaced previous tribunals and established the First-tier Tribunal and the Upper Tribunal.

There are four chambers, the Administrative Appeals Chambers, the Tax and Chamber, the Lands Chamber and the Immigration and Asylum Chamber.

The Upper Tribunal is a superior court of record albeit the jurisdiction in respect of contempt is more circumscribed.

The First-tier Tribunal is an inferior court of record. The procedure for its contempt powers is by way of making an application to the Divisional Court. The Rules of the Supreme Court Order 52 refers. In **Peach and Grey and Co v Sommers** [1995] 2 ALL ER 513, the Divisional Court dealt specifically with employment tribunals and that it was an inferior court of record. The Divisional Court went on to pass a sentence of one month for the contempt of court.

A recent example of the Upper Tribunal dealing with a potential contempt case is **Heal v The Chancellor, Masters and Scholars of the University of Oxford and others** UKEAT/01831/19DA, [2020] 2 WLUK 59. Mr Justice Choudhury, the President of the Employment Appeal Tribunal, dealt with an appeal against an applicant's request to use recording equipment in a hearing connected to his learning disabilities. The issue being that in most circumstances the unauthorised use of recording equipment in court proceedings would be a contempt of court.

Choudhury J in a clear judgment explained that in appropriate limited cases, permission can be granted for the use of recording equipment, but with sufficient safeguards. He said,

> *"Permission to record proceedings is unlikely to be granted on a routine or regular basis. Each case will have to be determined on its own facts. However, it seems very unlikely that permission would be granted where the applicant fails to demonstrate that, for reasons related to a disability or medical condition:*

i. there is a complete or partial inability to take contemporaneous notes; and

ii. such inability will result, in the circumstances of the particular case, in a substantial disadvantage."

Magistrates Courts

Magistrates Courts get their contempt powers from section 12 of the Contempt of Court Act 1981.

CHAPTER SEVEN

THE INITIAL STEPS IN CONTEMPT PROCEEDINGS

Many efforts to enforce orders by committal fail because of procedural impropriety. There has to be strict compliance with procedure and service. The fact that the Defendant's liberty is at risk requires no less.

Noting that CPR Part 81 and FPR Part 37 are in similar terms. Various missteps can arise. A step-by-step approach will assist.

Step 1: Consider the parties, their ages and capacity.

Check the defendant's date of birth.

Those under 18 cannot be committed to any form of detention. See s1(1) of Criminal Justice Act 1981 and **Mason v Lawton** [1991] 2 FLR 50.

Check that there are no issues in respect of the defendant's mental capacity.

The Court of Appeal's judgment in **Wookey v Wookey** [1991] 3 WLR 135 makes clear that a person who is not capable of understanding an injunction cannot be found to be in contempt by disobeying that injunction.

Proceedings relating to such persons are referred to as protected parties. The Mental Capacity Act 2005 has heralded a busy new regime mainly within the Court of Protection, but also via the High Court's retained inherent jurisdiction to deal the important rights of those who might lack capacity.

The principles from the Mental Capacity Act 2005 are set out in clear terms. The most important including that a person is assumed to have capacity. Therefore, just because the person might have made an unwise decision, does not mean that they lack capacity.

Section 1 MCA explains (emphasis added),

"1 The principles

(1) The following principles apply for the purposes of this Act.

*(2) **<u>A person must be assumed to have capacity unless it is established that he lacks capacity.</u>***

(3) A person is not to be treated as unable to make a decision unless all practicable steps to help him to do so have been taken without success.

*(4) **<u>A person is not to be treated as unable to make a decision merely because he makes an unwise decision.</u>***

(5) An act done, or decision made, under this Act for or on behalf of a person who lacks capacity must be done, or made, in his best interests.

(6) Before the act is done, or the decision is made, regard must be had to whether the purpose for which it is needed can be as effectively achieved in a way that is less restrictive of the person's rights and freedom of action."

Section 2 makes clear that it is not sufficient to assume that a person lacks capacity just because of their age or appearance.

Section 4 MCA refers to 'best interests'. In reality section 4 states that the full background is to be taken into account about the person and the issues when seeking to decide what might in the person's best interests. Section 4 states,

"4 Best interests

(1) In determining for the purposes of this Act what is in a person's best interests, the person making the determination must not make it merely on the basis of–

(a) the person's age or appearance, or

(b) a condition of his, or an aspect of his behaviour, which might lead others to make unjustified assumptions about what might be in his best interests.

(2) The person making the determination must consider all the relevant circumstances and, in particular, take the following steps.

(3) He must consider–

(a) whether it is likely that the person will at some time have capacity in relation to the matter in question, and

(b) if it appears likely that he will, when that is likely to be.

(4) He must, so far as reasonably practicable, permit and encourage the person to participate, or to improve his ability to participate, as fully as possible in any act done for him and any decision affecting him.

(5) Where the determination relates to life-sustaining treatment he must not, in considering whether the treatment is in the best interests of the person concerned, be motivated by a desire to bring about his death.

(6) He must consider, so far as is reasonably ascertainable–

(a) the person's past and present wishes and feelings (and, in particular, any relevant written statement made by him when he had capacity),

(b) the beliefs and values that would be likely to influence his decision if he had capacity, and

(c) the other factors that he would be likely to consider if he were able to do so.

(7) He must take into account, if it is practicable and appropriate to consult them, the views of–

(a) anyone named by the person as someone to be consulted on the matter in question or on matters of that kind,

(b) anyone engaged in caring for the person or interested in his welfare,

(c) any donee of a lasting power of attorney granted by the person, and

(d) any deputy appointed for the person by the court,

as to what would be in the person's best interests and, in particular, as to the matters mentioned in subsection (6).

(8) The duties imposed by subsections (1) to (7) also apply in relation to the exercise of any powers which–

> *(a) are exercisable under a lasting power of attorney, or*
>
> *(b) are exercisable by a person under this Act where he reasonably believes that another person lacks capacity.*
>
> *(9) In the case of an act done, or a decision made, by a person other than the court, there is sufficient compliance with this section if (having complied with the requirements of subsections (1) to (7)) he reasonably believes that what he does or decides is in the best interests of the person concerned.*
>
> *(10) "Life-sustaining treatment" means treatment which in the view of a person providing health care for the person concerned is necessary to sustain life.*
>
> *(11) "Relevant circumstances" are those–*
>
> *(a) of which the person making the determination is aware, and*
>
> *(b) which it would be reasonable to regard as relevant."*

Wookey v Wookey is an important case and was brought to counsels' attention by Cobb J in a recent MCA 2005 case dealing with the inherent jurisdiction of the High Court relating to vulnerable adults. In **Redcar and Cleveland Borough Council v PR and others** [2019] EWHC 2305 (Fam) Cobb J explained,

> *"23. Prompted by my specific enquiry, all counsel addressed me on the relevance to these facts of the decision of Wookey v Wookey [1991] 3 WLR 135 . This was a case of a husband ("H") appealing against domestic violence orders and orders under the Matrimonial Homes Act 1983 . The orders sought to prevent the husband from returning to his matrimonial home where his wife ("W") lived. H was suffering from the effects of early onset dementia and pathological jealousy which would cause him to attack his elderly wife. H had been admitted to hospital under s.2 Mental Health Act 1983 and the principle to be considered was whether an individual without mental capacity should be made subject to injunctive orders. The court held that H should not be subject to such an order and the appeal was upheld.*
>
> *24. In a passage in Wookey v Wookey which has obvious resonance here, Butler-Sloss LJ referred (at p.141) to the importance of the*

respondent understanding the proceedings and the nature and requirements of the order sought. Taken as a whole, the case of Wookey v Wookey established the following principles of relevance to the instant facts:

i) the equitable discretionary remedy of an injunction was a remedy in personam granted only against those who were amenable to the court's jurisdiction;

ii) in the case of mental incapacity, the question was whether the respondent understood the nature and requirements of the order sought;

iii) an injunction ought not to be granted against someone found within the M'Naughton Rules as he is incapable of understanding what he is doing or that what he is doing is wrong; it would not achieve the desired deterrent effect nor would it act to control a person's conduct and any breach of the order could not be effectively enforced; (Butler-Sloss LJ: "An injunction should not, therefore, be granted to impose an obligation to do something which is impossible or cannot be enforced. The injunction must serve a useful purpose for the person seeking the relief and there must be a real possibility that the order, if made, will be enforceable by the process in personam *");*

iv) balancing the protection of W against the disability by reason of mental incapacity of H, and in light of the powers available under the 1983 Act , it was inappropriate to grant the injunction.

25. It will be reasonably apparent that Wookey v Wookey lends some support to [Counsel for PR's] argument. What the Local Authority and/or court could or should have done, she submits, would have been to join SR and TR to the process from the outset, and for the court to have made the injunctive order against them at that stage. "

Cobb J went on to refer to **Wookey v Wookey** in the following terms,

"To some extent, the appropriateness of this type of provision will always be a question of fact and degree. As Butler-Sloss LJ said in Wookey :

> *"If it is clear that he is mentally ill, the extent of his ability to understand becomes crucial. If he may well understand the purpose of an injunction, no problem arises, and an interim order might be made whilst waiting for evidence " (emphasis added) (at p.143)"*

Step 2. Consider the type of contempt proceedings. Is permission to bring proceedings required?

If it is a civil/family contempt case, is permission required to bring contempt proceedings? You will need to consider the public interest committal test if it is.

In summary, [see CPR 81.3(5) and FPR 37.3 (5)] permission to make the contempt of court application is required if it is to deal with an allegation of:

(1) Contempt arising out of the due administration of justice; or

(2) Making a false statement in a document signed with a statement of truth

TBD (Owen Holland) Ltd v Simons and others [2021] 1 WLR 992 is a Court of Appeal case. The report is over 200 pages. It is an excellent judgment. The appeal dealt with search orders (the history of **Anton Piller** orders) in commercial cases, but also with committal matters and the issue of permission to bring contempt proceedings.

Arnold LJ, with whom the rest of the Court of Appeal agreed, provided the main reasoned judgment. It is of some importance and requires paragraph 230 onwards to be referred to.

> *"230. I turn now to the second principal issue raised by these appeals, which is the granting of permission to bring applications for committal, in particular applications for committal for making false statements pursuant to CPR r 81.17. (At the time of writing this judgment, Part 81 has just been substantially revised, but I am of course referring to the provisions as they stood at the material times.)*

231. A procedural question which was not canvassed during the course of argument, and only occurred to me when writing this judgment, is whether the court's permission is also required to bring applications for committal for swearing a false affidavit. In the case of applications for committal for breaching a court order, permission is not required: see rule 81.12(1), (3). In Hydropool Hot Tubs v RoberJot [2011] EWHC 121 (Ch) at [58]–[60] I held that what was then rule 32.14 did not apply to affidavits, and this was followed in relation to rules 81.17(4)(a) and 81.18(1)(a), (3)(a) by Green J in International Sports Tours Ltd (trading as Inspire Sports) v Shorey [2015] EWHC 2040 (QB) at [39]–[42]. It is arguable, however, that the effect of rule 81.12(1), (3) is nevertheless to require permission. Fortunately, it is not necessary to reach a conclusion on this point. Either way, TBD could have brought an application for the committal of Mr Simons without the court's permission on at least ground 1 (breaching the 4 July 2018 Order) even if it required permission to do so on ground 2 (swearing a false affidavit) as well as on ground 3 (making a false statement of truth in his defence). Similarly, TBD did not need the permission of the court to apply for Mr O'Boyle's committal on ground 1 alleged against him even if required permission to do so on grounds 2 and 4 as well as on grounds 3 and 5.

232. Turning to the approach which the court should adopt to an application for permission under rule 81.17, the leading authority is the judgment of Moore-Bick LJ in KJM Superbikes Ltd v Hinton (Practice Note) [2009] 1 WLR 2406. The guidance in that judgment was helpfully distilled by Hooper LJ in Barnes (trading as Pool Motors) v Seabrook [2010] CP Rep 42 in a passage at para 41 which was cited by Christopher Clarke LJ in Cavendish Square Holdings BV v Makdessi (No 2) [2013] EWCA Civ 1540 at [28]:

"(i) A person who makes a statement verified with a statement of truth or a false disclosure statement is only guilty of contempt if the statement is false and the person knew it to be so when he made it.

"(ii) It must be in the public interest for proceedings to be brought. In deciding whether it is in the public interest, the following factors are relevant: (a) the case against the alleged contemnor must be a strong case (there is an obvious need to

guard carefully against the risk of allowing vindictive litigants to use such proceedings to harass persons against whom they have a grievance); (b) the false statements must have been significant in the proceedings; (c) the court should ask itself whether the alleged contemnor understood the likely effect of the statement and the use to which it would be put in the proceedings; (d) 'the pursuit of contempt proceedings in ordinary cases may have a significant effect by drawing the attention of the legal profession, and through it that of potential witnesses, to the dangers of making false statements. If the courts are seen to treat serious examples of false evidence as of little importance, they run the risk of encouraging witnesses to regard the statement of truth as a mere formality.'

"(iii) The court must give reasons but be careful to avoid prejudicing the outcome of the substantive proceedings.

"(iv) Only limited weight should be attached to the likely penalty.

"(v) A failure to warn the alleged contemnor at the earliest opportunity of the fact that he may have committed a contempt is a matter that the court may take into account."

233. I would add two points to this summary. The first is the point made by David Richards J (as he then was) in Daltel Europe Ltd v Makki [2005] EWHC 749 (Ch) at [80] and cited with approval by Moore-Bick LJ in KJM at para 18:

"Allegations that statements of case and witness statements contain deliberately false statements are by no means uncommon and, in a fair number of cases, the allegations are well-founded. ***If parties thought that they could gain an advantage by singling out these statements and making them the subject of a committal application, the usual process of litigation would be seriously disrupted.*** *In general the proper time for determining the truth or falsity of these statements is at trial, when all the relevant issues of fact are before the court and the statements can be considered against the totality of the evidence. Further, the court will then decide all the issues according to the civil standard of proof and will not be applying the*

criminal standard to isolated issues, as must happen on an application under CPR Pt 32.14 ."

234. The second is the point made by Christopher Clarke LJ in Cavendish Square [2013] EWCA Civ 1540 at [79]:

"The critical question, in this and every case, is whether or not it is in the public interest that an application to commit should be made. That is not an issue of fact but a question of judgment. The discretion to permit an application to commit should be approached with considerable caution. It is not in the public interest that applications to commit should become a regular feature in cases where at or shortly before trial it appears that statements of fact in pleadings supported by statements of truth may have been untrue."

A recent example of permission being was refused is a judgment of Steyn J in **Gavigan v Norton** [2020] EWHC 2583 QB. That decision also deals succinctly with the issue of 'satellite litigation'. Steyn J said (emphasis has been added),

"50. My conclusion that there is not a strong prima facie case is sufficient to lead to the conclusion that the application should be dismissed. However, I consider that there are additional reasons to dismiss this application:

i) **First, I do not consider that satellite litigation by means of a committal application would be proportionate.** It is highly undesirable that at the same time as the main proceedings are being determined before the County Court there should be an outstanding committal application before the High Court against Mrs Norton. **Committal proceedings would be an undesirable and unnecessary interference with the main proceedings, obstructing the disposal of what remains outstanding between the parties.**

ii) Secondly, there is a risk that this application may be being brought or supported out of a vindictive desire to harass Mrs Norton. The Claimant's argument laid emphasis on a desire that Mrs Norton be punished " ***preferably by way of imprisonment***

> ***rather than fine*** **" (albeit the Claimant submitted that what form of punishment, and in particular whether any term of imprisonment should be suspended, would be a matter for the committal hearing).** Mrs Norton's evidence is that the claim for an account was served on her on the first anniversary of her late husband's death and that Stephen Norton said to her **in September 2016 that he would "** ***spend whatever it takes*** **" to destroy her.** There is no apparent motive, on the evidence before me, for funding the main proceedings and this application other than to continue a feud against his stepmother by proxy. **It would be contrary to the public interest to allow the court's processes to be used oppressively**.
>
> *51. **In the circumstances, the overriding objective would not be furthered by granting permission.**"*

Civil Contempt- Other examples for judgments including abuse of process and the role of the claimants

In **Berry Piling Systems Ltd v Sheer Projects Ltd** [2013] EWHC 340 (TCC) Akenhead J dealt with permission applications to commence committal proceedings. His Lordship set out in clear terms as follows,

> *"30. These five elements (strong prima facie case, not straying into the merits, public interest, proportionality and overriding objective) have been adopted by the editors of the White Book and I accept that this is and should be the right approach. I add these further observations:*
>
> *(a) It is not enough for there to be merely a prima facie case; it must be a strong case. Without straying into the merits, the judge can, as the Court in Malgar and Kirk did, review critically the evidence to satisfy himself or herself that there is such a case.*
>
> *(b) It can be said that the strong prima facie case requirement is a primary one because there is often a public interest in a given case (and as a matter of deterrence) to pursue people who it strongly appears have deliberately misled the Court and where such misleading may well have led to an interference with justice. This requirement may often overlap in fact with one or more of the other requirements.*

(c) Optimism or even carelessness in the making of statements particularly in the case of value judgement type statements will not be sufficient to establish that a party deliberately or recklessly made a misstatement.

(d) As to proportionality in the exercise of the Court's discretion, it is not possible to give some blanket definition as to the factors to take into account as circumstances will vary widely. One can however have regard, amongst many other factors, to the strength of the case against the particular respondents, the amounts in money terms which were involved in the proceedings in which the allegedly false statement was made and which were affected by such statement, the likely costs involved or to be involved on both sides in the pursuant contempt proceedings and the court time likely to be involved in the case managing and hearing the matter. In doing this exercise, one must have regard to the overriding objective."

More recently the Court of Appeal in **Ocado Group Plc & Another v Raymond John McKeeve** [2021] EWCA Civ 145 dealt with an appeal from the decision of Marcus Smith J when he had refused Ocado's application to bring contempt proceedings connected to the due administration of justice. It will be remembered that Ocado is the company that had been undertaking house food deliveries on behalf of Waitrose for many years and was then to commence an online delivery service for Marks and Spencer instead. As Davis LJ explained, this was a "remarkable case" in which a solicitor was alleged to have said 'burn it all' following a court order which had required that and other evidence to be preserved. Davis LJ said,

"2. The context of the contempt application is, on any view, remarkable. It is admitted that within minutes of being notified of the fact that an Order for Search of Premises and Preservation of Evidence had been made in the High Court against clients of his, Mr McKeeve, a solicitor, gave instructions to his clients' Information Technology manager to "Burn it" (or "Burn all"). In consequence, that manager then deleted or disabled various IT accounts. One of these was an account, previously operated on a covert basis, known as the 3CX account. Its deletion has meant that any messages sent via that account are wholly irretrievable.

> ***Ocado has alleged that Mr McKeeve's conduct was intended to interfere with the due administration of justice."***

The Court of Appeal allowed the appeal with Davis LJ concluding,

> ***"61. In the present case, I am in no doubt at all, with all respect to the judge, that he reached a conclusion which was plainly wrong. Indeed such a conclusion would seem to set at a premium, where litigation is under way, the deliberate and irretrievable destruction of documents so that it is then asserted that no one can say for sure what they contained. No court can or should readily countenance that."***

It is important though for any Court considering a contempt application to ensure that the claimant is not using the contempt process as an abuse of process or for improper purposes. It is also important that the Court reminds the claimant that the claimant has a quasi-prosecutor role.

In **Navigator Equities Limited and Vladimir Anatolevich Chernukhin v Oleg Vladimirovich Deripaska** [2020] EWHC 1798 (Comm)[7] Andrew Baker J set out in a detailed judgment the background to the dispute involving very large sums of money. He also dealt with the contempt issues relating to undertakings which had been given by the Defendant.

His Lordship considered the role of the claimant in applications for contempt and whether there had been an abuse of process in the application before him. He said,

> *"At all events in those particular circumstances of this case, I am persuaded that it was incumbent on the claimants to prosecute the contempt application dispassionately as guardians of the public interest.*
>
> *4. I find that the claimants have not done so in respects that, in my view, render the process they have chosen to conduct unfair to the defendant. For that and other reasons, in my judgment the proper inference to draw is, and I find, that the contempt application was*

[7] On appeal to the Court of Appeal

issued and has been pursued by the claimants out of and in pursuit of the second claimant's deep-rooted personal animosity towards the defendant.

....as I can see from the claimants' skeleton argument, and will no doubt be presented orally by Mr Mill QC assuming the damages claim is pursued, so far as the contempt application is concerned in my judgment that argument has been and is being deployed by the claimants to vex and harass the defendant, not in order to draw serious misconduct to the attention of the court so as to allow the court to take its own view on what, if any, sanction it should attract in the public interest.

...I conclude that this contempt application is an abuse of the court's process and it must be dismissed."

His Lordship went on to say,

"A Quasi-Prosecution

138. A contempt application may be struck out if brought for an improper purpose. Indeed, as it was put by Briggs J, as he was then, in Sectorguard plc v Dienne plc [2009] EWHC 2693 (Ch) at [53], contempt proceedings in relation to alleged breaches of an injunction or undertaking may be struck out as abusive if brought " otherwise than for the legitimate motive of seeking enforcement [of the injunction or undertaking], or bringing to the court's attention a serious rather than purely technical contempt ". Thus, for example;

(i) " *The court should be astute to detect when contempt proceedings are not being pursued for legitimate aims* ", *per* Hamblen J, as he was then, in *PJSC Vseukrainskyi Aktsionernyi Bank v Maksimov [2014] EWHC 4370 (Comm)* at [22].

(ii) " *There is an obvious need to guard carefully against the risk of allowing vindictive litigants to use such proceedings to harass persons against whom they have a grievance, whether justified or not ...* ", *per* Moore-Bick LJ in *KJM Superbikes Ltd v Hinton [2009] 1 WLR 2406* at [17].

(iii) Most simply, " *an application must not be brought for an illegitimate purpose* ", *per* Sir Michael Burton in Super Max v Malhotra [2019] EWHC 2711 (Comm) at [10].

142. One consequence I have already identified, namely that the court recognises the particular capacity of contempt applications or the threat of contempt applications to be used vexatiously by litigants to further interests that it is not the function of the contempt jurisdiction to serve…

143. A further consequence is that the claimant / applicant pursues a contempt charge as much as quasi-prosecutor serving the public interest as it does as private litigant pursuing its own interests in the underlying dispute. The claimant / applicant needs to understand that; and if it is legally represented, as here, the legal representatives need to understand that their role as officers of the court is acutely pertinent, even if (to repeat) the process is not to be equated with a private prosecution in a criminal court. Thus, it appears to have struck Teare J as obvious in the long-running Ablyazov litigation that the quasi-prosecutorial role of the claimant / applicant in pursuing a contempt charge means its proper function is to act generally dispassionately, to present the facts fairly and with balance, and then let those facts speak for themselves, assisting the court to make a fair quasi-criminal judgment: JSC BTA Bank v Ablyazov [2012] EWHC 237 (Comm) at [15].

145. The only proper purpose that might be served by issuing and prosecuting the contempt application, in those circumstances, was so as to invite the court in the public interest to identify, pronounce and punish, if appropriate, an historic contempt. The contempt application ought to have been pursued dispassionately by the claimants as parties with no interest in the outcome. It was instead pursued in aggressive, partisan fashion, as if it were just the latest round in this long-running, 'no-holds barred', commercial litigation wrestling match… His was therefore a paradigm example of a case where an alleged contemnor needed the protection of a scrupulously careful and even-handed prosecution of the charge against him.

The Abuse

154. Adopting the approach, then, that this contempt application ought to have been prosecuted dispassionately and even-handedly as an application brought solely in the public interest and not to serve any partisan agenda of the claimants', and that particular care was called for not to allow an appearance of unfairness to be created because of what was said in court on 3 July 2019, I can now set out the features that I concluded had come together to render the application an abuse of the process of the court…

156. Secondly, the claimants' evidence in support of the contempt charge was in material respects misleading or not the whole truth, or both of those together...

157. Thirdly, there is real reason to suppose that Mr Chernukhin instructed Clifford Chance to issue and pursue the contempt charge as an act of revenge for Mr Deripaska's twin moves in May 2019…

158. Fourthly, the contempt application was presented to the court in a heavy-handed, aggressively partisan fashion, that was inappropriate, vexatious and unfair…

His Lordship noted the increase in hostility in commercial cases (which in my view is the same across many areas of law) and he said in stark terms (emphasis added),

"161. In the working generation of 30 years or so during which I have been engaged in commercial dispute resolution in this jurisdiction, principally in this court and in London arbitrations, there has been a significant general increase in hostility and aggressiveness in the conduct of disputes. The taking of any and every point, good or bad, and other failures to display proper independence from the litigating client, is treated too often as if it were a normal or appropriate adjunct of well funded, hard fought, business disputes, particularly if there are issues of dishonesty involved. Where ultimately the court is asked only to decide the outcome of the business dispute, usually to be expressed in terms of a party or parties being told to pay money to another party or other parties, there may be nothing too unfair about that modern style, regrettable though I regard it nonetheless. ***But when the court is***

> ***being asked by a private litigant to consider a charge of contempt of court against the other side, especially against an individual whose liberty the applicant therefore seeks to put at risk, a better standard of conduct is not merely desirable, it is essential to the fairness and the appearance of fairness of the process.*** *Though I do not suppose that this is how the claimants' legal team saw what they were doing, the appearance in this case was of claimants not seeking to put Mr Deripaska fairly on trial for contempt, but of claimants seeking to load the dice against him."*

CHAPTER EIGHT

PROCEDURE

Further Procedure and Burden and Standard of Proof

It is a fundamental principle that the Claimant has the burden of proving the allegations in its contempt application. The Claimant must prove those allegations to the criminal standard of proof. Put another way, it remains for the Claimant to satisfy the Court that it is sure that the Defendant has breached the order or undertakings.

This brings with it consideration of mens rea usually seen in the criminal courts.[8]

On a contempt application for breach of a court order, the claimant had to prove to the criminal standard that the defendant had the necessary mens rea. Where the defendant said that compliance with the order had been impossible, and there was some evidence in support, mens rea was in issue and the claimant had to prove to the criminal standard that compliance had been possible.

CPR Part 81 and FPR Part 37 are in similar terms. Both are set out below, but a judgment of the Court of Appeal in **Andreewitch v Moutreuil** [2020] EWCA Civ 282, [2020] 4 WLR 54 provides an important checklist albeit it is a judgment from before the introduction of CPR 81 and FPR 37.

---

[8] See **Perkier Foods Ltd v Halo Foods Ltd and another** [2019] EWHC 3462 in which Chamberlain J considered this issue. On a committal application for breach of a court order, the claimant had to prove to the criminal standard that the defendant had the necessary mens rea. Where the defendant said that compliance with the order had been impossible, and there was some evidence in support, mens rea was in issue and the claimant had to prove to the criminal standard that compliance had been possible.

Peter Jackson LJ with whom Popplewell LJ agreed set out in detail the following matters (emphasis has been added),

> *15. **Proceedings for contempt of court are unlike ordinary civil or family proceedings in that they may lead to the imposition of a punishment. For that reason special safeguards exist for the benefit of the respondent/defendant. At the same time, the overall objective is fairness, and in seeking to achieve that the court must take into account the interests of all parties and the public interest in the maintenance of the authority of the court.** That approach, which is common across all subject jurisdictions, is reflected in FPR PD37 13.2 and CPR PD81 16.2 which permit, but do not require, the court to waive any procedural defect in the commencement or conduct of a committal application if satisfied that no injustice has been caused. Accordingly, while it is of great importance that the procedural rules are complied with, the process will not be invalidated on (to borrow from the White Book) purely technical grounds that have nothing to do with the justice of the case. As was said in Yaxley-Lennon , a balance must be struck where the relevant rules have not been followed to the letter.*

> *16. **The starting point when striking the balance in this case is the duty upon a court hearing committal proceedings to ensure that the accused person is made aware that they are not obliged to give evidence and also warned that adverse consequences or inferences may arise from exercising the right to silence.** Those messages may indeed contain a tension, but what matters is **that the choice of how to proceed belongs to the litigant and not to the other party or to the court. This is of particular importance when the litigant is unrepresented,** and it does not apply any the less to the seasoned litigant in person, or to the litigant who appears eager to enter the witness box. The last mentioned individual may be the one who most needs to be reminded of his or her rights.*

> *17. I therefore do not accept the argument that there was no procedural defect in what occurred in this case. I reject the submission that PA can be taken to have been informed of his rights by the reference to the rules in the skeleton argument. Even if that went some small way to informing him of where he stood, it was undone by the events at the*

hearing, as described at paragraph 5 above. Likewise, I cannot accept the description of this breach as being a purely technical one. The right to silence is a core element in criminal proceedings and proceedings of a criminal character.

*18. **That being the case, the decision can only stand if we are satisfied that no injustice has been caused. There is a temptation to reason that the case brought by MM was on the face of it a strong one, that in the absence of a good explanation from PA it was likely to be proved, that PA is an able litigant in person who accepted the suggestion that he give evidence with alacrity, and that the outcome may well have been the same whether or not he gave oral evidence.** I am not persuaded by these arguments…*

*20…**Put another way, there has been a serious procedural irregularity that justifies the grant of permission to appeal and the allowing of the appeal on this ground. In the circumstances the other grounds of appeal fall away and I say nothing about them…***

*22. …**This court was referred to the checklist contained in paragraph 78 of the judgment of Theis J in Re L (see below) and I have no doubt that if the judge had had the same benefit, this appeal would not have arisen.***

> ***"78. Before any court embarks on hearing a committal application, whether for a contempt in the face of the court or for breach of an order, it should ensure that the following matters are at the forefront of its mind:***
>
> ***(1) There is complete clarity at the start of the proceedings as to precisely what the foundation of the alleged contempt is: contempt in the face of the court, or breach of an order.***
>
> ***(2) Prior to the hearing the alleged contempt should be set out clearly in a document or application that complies with FPR rule 37 and which the person accused of contempt has been served with.***
>
> ***(3) If the alleged contempt is founded on breach of a previous court order, the person accused had been served with that***

order, and that it contained a penal notice in the required form and place in the order.

(4) Whether the person accused of contempt has been given the opportunity to secure legal representation, as they are entitled to.

(5) Whether the judge hearing the committal application should do so, or whether it should be heard by another judge.

(6) Whether the person accused of contempt has been advised of the right to remain silent.

(7) If the person accused of contempt chooses to give evidence, whether they have been warned about self-incrimination.

(8) The need to ensure that in order to find the breach proved the evidence must meet the criminal standard of proof, of being sure that the breach is established.

(9) Any committal order made needs to set out what the findings are that establish the contempt of court, which are the foundation of the court's decision regarding any committal order.

79. Counsel and solicitors are reminded of their duty to assist the court. This is particularly important when considering procedural matters where a person's liberty is at stake.""

I set out above FPR Part 37 and the reference to contempt. As was said there, the CPR Part 81 is in similar terms and has been borrowed from it. I now set out CPR Part 81 too. I have added the emphasis in bold to ease reading.

PART 81 – Applications and Proceedings in Relation to Contempt of Court

Scope

81.1

(1) This Part sets out the procedure to be followed in proceedings for contempt of court ("contempt proceedings").

(2) This Part does not alter the scope and extent of the jurisdiction of courts determining contempt proceedings, whether inherent, statutory or at common law.

(3) **This Part has effect subject to and to the extent that it is consistent with the substantive law of contempt of court.**

Interpretation

81.2

In this Part—

"claimant" means a person making a contempt application;

"contempt application" means an application to the court for an order determining contempt proceedings;

"defendant" means the person against whom the application is made;

"order of committal" means the imposition of a sentence of imprisonment (whether immediate or suspended) for contempt of court;

"penal notice" means a prominent notice on the front of an order warning that if the person against whom the order is made (and, in the case of a corporate body, a director or officer of that body) disobeys the court's order, the person (or director or officer) may be held in contempt of court and punished by a fine, imprisonment, confiscation of assets or other punishment under the law.

How to make a contempt application

81.3

(1) **A contempt application made in existing High Court or county court proceedings is made by an application under Part 23 in those proceedings, whether or not the application is made against a party to those proceedings.**

(2) **If the application is made in the High Court, it shall be determined by a High Court judge of the Division in which the case is proceeding. If it is made in the county court, it shall be determined by a Circuit Judge sitting in the county court, unless under a rule or practice direction it may be determined by a District Judge.**

(3) A contempt application in relation to **alleged interference with the due administration of justice, otherwise than in existing High Court or county court proceedings, is made by an application to the High Court under Part 8.**

(4) Where an application under Part 8 is made under paragraph (3), the rules in Part 8 apply except as modified by this Part and the defendant is not required to acknowledge service of the application.

(5) **Permission to make a contempt application** is required where the application is made in relation to—

(a) interference with the due administration of justice, except in relation to existing High Court or county court proceedings;

(b) an allegation of knowingly making a false statement in any affidavit, affirmation or other document verified by a statement of truth or in a disclosure statement.

(6) **If permission to make the application is needed, the application for permission shall be included in the contempt application,** which will proceed to a full hearing only if permission is granted.

(7) If permission is needed and the application relates to High Court proceedings, the question of permission shall be determined by a single judge of the Division in which the case is proceeding. If permission is granted the contempt application shall be determined by a single judge or Divisional Court of that Division.

(8) **If permission is needed and the application does not relate to existing court proceedings or relates to criminal or county court proceedings or to proceedings in the Civil Division of the Court of Appeal, the question of permission shall be determined by a single judge of the Queen's Bench Division.** If permission is granted, the contempt application shall be determined by a single judge of the Queen's Bench Division or a Divisional Court.

Requirements of a contempt application

81.4

(1) Unless and to the extent that the court directs otherwise, **every contempt application must be supported by written evidence given by affidavit or affirmation.**

(2) **A contempt application must include statements** of all the following, unless (in the case of (b) to (g)) wholly inapplicable—

(a) **the nature of the alleged contempt (for example, breach of an order or undertaking or contempt in the face of the court);**

(b) **the date and terms of any order allegedly breached or disobeyed;**

(c) **confirmation that any such order was personally served, and the date it was served, unless the court or the parties dispensed with personal service;**

(d) **if the court dispensed with personal service, the terms and date of the court's order dispensing with personal service;**

(e) confirmation that any order allegedly breached or disobeyed included a penal notice;

(f) the date and terms of any undertaking allegedly breached;

(g) confirmation of the claimant's belief that the person who gave any undertaking understood its terms and the consequences of failure to comply with it;

(h) a brief summary of the facts alleged to constitute the contempt, set out numerically in chronological order;

(i) that the defendant has the right to be legally represented in the contempt proceedings;

(j) that the defendant is entitled to a reasonable opportunity to obtain legal representation and to apply for legal aid which may be available without any means test;

(k) that the defendant may be entitled to the services of an interpreter;

(l) that the defendant is entitled to a reasonable time to prepare for the hearing;

(m)that the defendant is entitled but not obliged to give written and oral evidence in their defence;

(n) that the defendant has the right to remain silent and to decline to answer any question the answer to which may incriminate the defendant;

(o)that the court may proceed in the defendant's absence if they do not attend but (whether or not they attend) will only find the defendant in contempt if satisfied beyond reasonable doubt of the facts constituting contempt and that they do constitute contempt;

(p)that if the court is satisfied that the defendant has committed a contempt, the court may punish the

defendant by a fine, imprisonment, confiscation of assets or other punishment under the law;

(q) that if the defendant admits the contempt and wishes to apologise to the court, that is likely to reduce the seriousness of any punishment by the court;

(r) that the court's findings will be provided in writing as soon as practicable after the hearing; and

(s) that the court will sit in public, unless and to the extent that the court orders otherwise, and that its findings will be made public.

Service of a contempt application

81.5

(1) Unless the court directs otherwise in accordance with Part 6 and except as provided in paragraph (2), a contempt application and evidence in support must be served on the defendant personally.

(2) Where a legal representative for the defendant is on the record in the proceedings in which, or in connection with which, an alleged contempt is committed–

(a) the contempt application and evidence in support may be served on the representative for the defendant unless the representative objects in writing within seven days of receipt of the application and evidence in support;

(b) if the representative does not object in writing, they must at once provide to the defendant a copy of the contempt application and the evidence supporting it and take all reasonable steps to ensure the defendant understands them;

(c) if the representative objects in writing, the issue of service shall be referred to a judge of the court dealing with the contempt application; and the judge shall consider written representations from the parties and determine the issue on the papers, without (unless the judge directs otherwise) an oral hearing.

Cases where no application is made

81.6

(1) If the court considers that a contempt of court (including a contempt in the face of the court) may have been committed, the court on its own initiative shall consider whether to proceed against the defendant in contempt proceedings.

(2) Where the court does so, any other party in the proceedings may be required by the court to give such assistance to the court as is proportionate and reasonable, having regard to the resources available to that party.

(3) If the court proceeds of its own initiative, it shall issue a summons to the defendant which includes the matters set out in rule 81.4(2)(a)-(s) (in so far as applicable) and requires the defendant to attend court for directions to be given.

(4) A summons issued under this rule shall be served on the defendant personally and on any other party, unless the court directs otherwise. If rule 81.5(2) applies, the procedure there set out shall be followed unless the court directs otherwise.

Directions for hearing of contempt proceedings

81.7

(1) The court shall give such directions as it thinks fit for the hearing and determination of contempt proceedings, including directions for the attendance of witnesses and oral evidence, as it considers appropriate.

(2) The court may issue a bench warrant to secure the attendance of the defendant at a directions hearing or at the substantive hearing.

(3) The court may not give any direction compelling the defendant to give evidence either orally or in writing.

Hearings and judgments in contempt proceedings

81.8

(1) In accordance with rule 39.2, all hearings of contempt proceedings shall, irrespective of the parties' consent, be listed and heard in public unless the court otherwise directs.

(2) Advocates and the judge shall appear robed in all hearings of contempt proceedings, whether or not the court sits in public.

(3) Before deciding to sit in private for all or part of the hearing, the court shall notify the national print and broadcast media, via the Press Association.

(4) The court shall consider any submissions from the parties or media organisations before deciding whether and if so to what extent the hearing should be in private.

(5) If the court decides to sit in private it shall, before doing so, sit in public to give a reasoned public judgment setting out why it is doing so.

(6) At the conclusion of the hearing, whether or not held in private, the court shall sit in public to give a reasoned public judgment stating its findings and any punishment.

(7) The court shall inform the defendant of the right to appeal without permission, the time limit for appealing and the court before which any appeal must be brought.

(8) The court shall be responsible for ensuring that judgments in contempt proceedings are transcribed and published on the website of the judiciary of England and Wales.

Powers of the court in contempt proceedings

81.9

(1) **If the court finds the defendant in contempt of court, the court may impose a period of imprisonment (an order of committal), a fine, confiscation of assets or other punishment permitted under the law.**

(2) Execution of an order of committal requires issue of a warrant of committal. An order of committal and a warrant of committal have immediate effect unless and to the extent that the court decides to suspend execution of the order or warrant.

(3) **An order or warrant of committal must be personally served on the defendant unless the court directs otherwise.**

(4) **To the extent that the substantive law permits, a court may attach a power of arrest to a committal order.**

(5) An order or warrant of committal may not be enforced more than two years after the date it was made unless the court directs otherwise.

Applications to discharge committal orders

81.10

(1) **A defendant against whom a committal order has been made may apply to discharge it.**

(2) **Any such application shall be made by an application notice under Part 23 in the contempt proceedings.**

(3) **The court hearing such an application shall consider all the circumstances and make such order under the law as it thinks fit.**

CHAPTER NINE

PENALTIES FOR CONTEMPT OF COURT

CPR Part 81.9 states that if the Court finds the Defendant in contempt of court then it can make an order of committal, including the imposition of a period of imprisonment for up to 2 years. For the Family Court, see FPR Part 37.9. This is a very important power which must be used carefully. CPR Part 81.9 states, (emphasis in bold has been added),

> (1) **If the court finds the defendant in contempt of court, the court may impose a period of imprisonment (an order of committal), a fine, confiscation of assets or other punishment permitted under the law.**
>
> (2) Execution of an order of committal requires issue of a warrant of committal. **An order of committal and a warrant of committal have immediate effect unless and to the extent that the court decides to suspend execution of the order or warrant.**
>
> (3) **An order or warrant of committal must be personally served on the defendant unless the court directs otherwise.**
>
> (4) To the extent that the substantive law permits, a court may attach a power of arrest to a committal order.
>
> (5) **An order or warrant of committal may not be enforced more than two years after the date it was made unless the court directs otherwise.**

In some cases, contemnors will refuse to attend hearings. If the contemnor has failed to attend the hearing, then the court can issue a bench warrant for his/her arrest. See **Frejeck v Frejeck** [2020] EWHC 1181 (Ch). The bench warrant enables the person to be apprehended by the police and then brought before the court.

The Court can hear the contempt case in the Defendant's absence, but must only do so with reluctance and care. See Cobb J in the family case (but which applies across all areas in my view) of **Sanchez v Oboz (Committal Proceedings in Absence of Respondents)** [2015] 235 (fam), [2016] 1 FLR 897. His Lordship set out a helpful checklist when deciding whether or not to proceed in the absence of Defendants (previously 'respondents'):

> i) Whether the respondents have been served with the relevant documents, including notice of this hearing;
>
> ii) Whether the respondents have had sufficient notice to enable them to prepare for the hearing;
>
> iii) Whether any reason has been advanced for their non-appearance;
>
> iv) Whether by reference to the nature and circumstances of the respondents' behaviour, they have waived their right to be present;
>
> v) Whether an adjournment would be likely to secure the attendance of the respondent or facilitate their representation;
>
> vi) The extent of the disadvantage to the respondents in not being able to present their account of events;
>
> vii) Whether undue prejudice would be caused to the applicant by any delay;
>
> viii) Whether undue prejudice would be caused to the forensic process if the application was to proceed in the absence of the respondents'
>
> ix) The terms of the 'overriding objective' under rule 1.1. FPR 2010"

The fact that the Court can sentence contemnors to imprisonment will usually carry considerable weight on the mind of those who might be tempted to breach court orders or undertakings. The deterrent effect of committal to prison is significant.

The court's power to punish for contempt of court may be exercised by an order for committal to prison, or by other means, such as an order requiring the contemnor to pay a fine or under which he or she gives security for good behaviour.

It is section 14 Contempt of Court Act 1981 that provides the court with that jurisdiction to sentence for contempt. The maximum period is 2 years on one occasion.

In **Liverpool Victoria Insurance Ltd v Zafar** [2019] EWCA Civ 392, [2019] 1 WLR 3833 the Court of Appeal gave important guidance on sentencing in contempt cases.

The court comprised Sir Thomas Etherton MR with Hamblin and Holroyde LJJ.

The judgment is a very useful reminder for sentencing purposes. It provides as follows (emphasis in bold has been added),

> ***"58. In the context of a contempt of court involving a false statement verified by a statement of truth, the contemnor may have acted dishonestly, or recklessly in the sense of not caring whether the statement was true or false. In either case, it is always serious, because it undermines the administration of justice. In considering just how serious it is in all the circumstances of an individual case, and in deciding the appropriate punishment for contempt of court, we think that the approach adopted by the criminal courts provides a useful comparison, though not a precise analogy. In particular, the Sentencing Council's definitive guidelines on the imposition of community and custodial sentences (see [30] above) and on reduction in sentence for a guilty plea are relevant in cases of this nature. It is therefore appropriate for a court dealing with this form of contempt of court to consider (as a criminal court would do) the culpability of the contemnor and the harm caused, intended or likely to be caused by the contempt of court. Having in that way determined the seriousness of the case, the court must consider whether a fine would be a sufficient penalty. If it would, committal to prison cannot be justified, even if the contemnor's means are so limited that the amount of the fine must be modest.***

> ***59. We say at once, however, that the deliberate or reckless making of a false statement in a document verified by a statement of truth will usually be so inherently serious that nothing other than an order for committal to prison will be sufficient. That is so whether the contemnor is a claimant seeking to support a spurious or exaggerated claim, a lay witness seeking to provide evidence in support of such a claim, or an expert witness putting forward an opinion without an honest belief in its truth. In the case of an expert witness, the fact that he or she is acting corruptly and makes the relevant false statement for reward, will make the case even more serious; but it will be a serious contempt of court even if the expert witness acts from an indirect financial motive*** *(such as a desire to obtain more work from a particular solicitor or claims manager), or without any financial motivation at all, and even if the expert witness stands to gain little financial reward by it. This is so because of the reliance placed on expert witnesses by the court, and because of the corresponding importance of the overriding duty which experts owe to the court (see [33-34] above).*
>
> ***60. Because this form of contempt of court undermines the administration of justice, it is always serious, even if the falsity of the relevant statement is identified at an early stage and does not in the end affect the outcome of the litigation. The fact that only a comparatively modest sum is claimed in the proceedings in which the false statement is made does not remove the seriousness of the contempt.*** *The sum in issue in the proceedings is however relevant, because contempt of court by an expert witness will be even more serious if the relevant false statement supports a claim for a large sum, or a sum which is grossly exaggerated above the true value of any legitimate claim.*
>
> ***61. As we have noted in [36] above, the essential feature of this form of contempt of court is the making of a false statement without an honest belief in its truth. In principle, where a false statement is made without an honest belief in its truth, a contemnor who acts recklessly is less culpable than one who acts intentionally. The extent of that difference in culpability will, however, depend on all the circumstances of the case. Without seeking to lay down an inflexible rule, we take the view that an***

expert witness who recklessly makes a false statement in a report or witness statement verified by a statement of truth will usually be almost as culpable as an expert witness who does so intentionally. *This is so, because the expert witness knows that the court and the parties are dependent on his or her being truthful, and has made a declaration which asserts that he or she is aware of his or her duties to the court and has complied with them (see [33] above). To abuse the trust placed in an expert witness by putting forward a statement which is in fact false, not caring whether it be true or not, is usually almost as serious a contempt of court as telling a deliberate lie.*

62. Moreover, as the present case illustrates, the culpability of a contemnor who acts recklessly will be increased if he or she knows of circumstances which cast doubt on the accuracy of the relevant statement, but nonetheless makes it without caring whether it be true or false. *When the Respondent made the first of the statements which the judge found to be false, only a week had passed since he had personally examined Mr Iqbal and found him to have made a full recovery. The Respondent therefore had good reason to question the claim of continuing pain which was now being put forward, and no obvious reason to think that he had himself made a mistake and had failed to notice or record those continuing symptoms. He nonetheless made a number of false statements without making any attempt to check their accuracy or to qualify them in any way. He made the declarations to which we have referred, and signed the statement of truth, when the contents of the revised report included (without attribution) something suggested to him by Mr Khan and was to that extent not based on his own independent view; and when the opinions which he expressed did not represent his "true and complete professional opinions" and were not his "completely independent opinion". In all the circumstances, his culpability in our view came close to that of an expert witness who deliberately made false statements. For that reason, we respectfully disagree with the judge's finding that the telling of one deliberate lie was the most serious aspect of the Respondent's conduct. The seriousness of the case lies, in our view, in the putting forward of the revised report as if it represented the Respondent's honest and independent opinion based upon his own examination of Mr Iqbal.*

63. Also relevant to the culpability of an expert witness who commits this form of contempt of court is the extent to which the witness persists in the false statement and/or resorts to other forms of misconduct in order to cover up the making of the false statement. *In the present case the judge found that the Respondent, having recklessly made a number of false statements in the revised report, tried to cover up what he had done by telling a direct lie in his witness statement of August 2013 and then recklessly made further false statements in advancing a different explanation in his witness statement of October 2013. In our view, the attempted cover-up, and the making of further false statements, significantly increased the Respondent's culpability.*

64. As we have indicated, an order for committal to prison will usually be inevitable where an expert witness commits this form of contempt of court, and counsel for the respondent realistically accepted that it was inevitable in this case. ***As to the appropriate length of sentence, it is important to emphasise that every case will turn on its particular facts.*** *The conduct involved in a contempt of this kind may vary across a wide range.* ***The court must, therefore, have in mind that the two year maximum term has to cater for that range of conduct, and must seek to impose a sentence in the instant case which sits appropriately within that range.*** *Where more than one contemnor is before the court, as in the present case, it will of course be necessary to make a judgment as to the comparative seriousness of their respective misconduct. As we have noted at [49] above, the Lord Chief Justice in* ***Bashir*** *had in mind as a starting point sentences "**well in excess of 12 months" even for those who played the role of "foot soldiers" in the dishonest claims in that case.***

65. In determining what is the least period of committal which properly reflects the seriousness of a contempt of court, the court must of course give due weight to ***matters of mitigation.*** *An early admission of the conduct constituting the contempt of court, before proceedings are commenced, will provide important mitigation, especially if it is volunteered before any allegation is made.* ***So too will cooperation*** *with any investigation into contempt of court committed by others involved in the same proceedings or in other fraudulent claims. Where the court is satisfied that the contemnor has shown* ***genuine remorse*** *for his or her conduct, that will provide mitigation. Serious ill health may be a factor properly taken into account.* ***Previous positive good character, an unblemished professional record and the fact that an expert witness has brought professional and financial ruin upon himself or herself are also matters which can be taken into account in the contemnor's favour.*** *However, in deciding what weight can be given to those matters, it must be remembered that it is the professional standing and good character of the expert witness which enables him or her to act as an expert witness, and thus to be in a position to make false statements of this kind.* ***Breach of the trust placed in an expert witness by the court must be expected to result in a severe sanction being imposed by the court in addition to any other adverse consequences.*** *The fact that an expert witness has brought ruin upon himself or herself, and/or the fact that he or she faces proceedings by a* ***professional disciplinary body, will therefore not in themselves be a reason not to impose a significant term of committal.***

66. The court must also give due weight to the ***impact of committal on persons other than the contemnor.*** *In particular, where the contemnor is the* ***sole or principal carer of children or vulnerable adults****, the court must ensure it is fully informed as to the consequences for those persons of the imprisonment of their carer. In a borderline case, such considerations may enable the court to avoid making an order for committal which would otherwise be made. In a case in which nothing less than an order for committal can be justified, the impact on others may provide a compelling reason to suspend its operation.*

67. As to delay, ***we think it important to distinguish unreasonable delay, not attributable to any fault on the part of the contemnor, from the passage of time which is a necessary consequence of the proper litigation of allegations of contempt of court.*** *Where a contemnor has made an early admission of wrongdoing, but for reasons beyond his or her control a long period of time then passes before a court imposes a sanction for the wrongdoing, the passage of time, attended as it inevitably would be by great anxiety, may be an important point in mitigation.* ***The position is, however, different when all wrongdoing is denied. An alleged contemnor is, of course,***

entitled to contest the allegation, and the fact that he or she does so cannot make the contempt more serious; but the contemnor cannot then expect much weight to be given *in his or her favour to the fact that the necessary court proceedings result in the passage of a substantial period of time. In the present case, a date for the trial of the contempt allegations was vacated because one of the other parties made a late application, and it is fair to say that the proceedings against the Respondent were thereby delayed for about 9 months. That was a point to which weight could be given in the Respondent's favour. However, it was in our view the only such point. Although it is unfortunate that the contempt proceedings took as long as they did, it was always open to the Respondent to try to shorten them by admitting his wrongdoing. He did not do so. We reject the submission on his behalf that he could not do so because he had to contest those allegations in respect of which he was successful: he could have made admissions regardless of whether the Appellant would regard them as sufficient, and, if he had done so, he would have had much stronger mitigation based on delay.*

68. Having reached a conclusion that a term of committal is inevitable, and having decided the appropriate length of that term, ***the court must consider what reduction should be made to reflect any admission of the contempt****. In this regard, the timing of the admission is important: the earlier an admission is made in the proceedings, the greater the reduction which will be appropriate.* ***Consistently with the approach taken in criminal cases pursuant to the Sentencing Council's definitive guideline, we think that a maximum reduction of one-third*** *(from the term reached after consideration of all relevant aggravating and mitigating features, including any admissions made before the commencement of proceedings) will only be appropriate where conduct constituting the contempt of court has been admitted as soon as proceedings are commenced.* ***Thereafter, any reduction should be on a sliding scale down to about 10% where an admission is made at trial.***

69. ***The court must, finally, consider whether the term of committal can properly be suspended.*** *In this regard, both principle and the caselaw to which we were referred lead to the conclusion that in the case of an expert witness, the appropriate term will usually have to be served immediately, and that one or more powerful factors* *justifying suspension will have to be shown if the term is to be suspended. We do not think that the court is necessarily precluded from taking into account, at this stage of the process, factors which have already been considered when deciding the appropriate length of the term of committal. Usually, however, the court in deciding the length of the term will already have given full weight to the mitigation, with the result that there is no powerful factor making it appropriate to suspend the term. If the immediate imprisonment of the contemnor will have a serious adverse effect on others, for example where the contemnor is the sole or principal carer of children or of vulnerable adults, that may make it appropriate for the term to be suspended; but even then, as Bashir shows, an immediate term – greatly shortened to reflect the personal mitigation – may well be necessary.*

70. We should add that we accept, as was submitted on behalf of the Appellant, that the fact that the relevant false statement was made recklessly rather than intentionally will not in itself usually be a powerful factor in favour of suspending the necessary term of committal.

71. It follows from all we have said about the approach to sentencing in cases of this nature, and about the limited grounds for interfering with a decision of this nature, ***that there will be few cases in which a decision as to the appropriate sentence for contempt will be open to challenge in this court, whether on grounds of undue leniency or of undue severity."***

Discharge of orders of committal to prison

The older authorities refer to a contemnor being able to 'purge' his or her contempt. The thinking being that once sent to prison and whilst in the cells, the contemnor will have reflected and seen how serious a position they had got themselves into.

The usual submission of counsel being that whether it is 14 days in prison or 3 months in prison, they both have the same effect of ensuring that there will be no repeat of the offending behaviour which had led to the order of committal to prison.

Whilst the old terminology of purging contempt is not now in use, the ability to seek to discharge committal orders prior to completing sentence is still permitted. The process do so is via a CPR Part 23 application with reference to CPR Part 81.10:

> ***81.10.— Applications to discharge committal orders***
>
> *(1) A defendant against whom a committal order has been made may apply to discharge it.*
>
> *(2) Any such application shall be made by an application notice under Part 23 in the contempt proceedings.*
>
> *(3) The court hearing such an application shall consider all the circumstances and make such order under the law as it thinks fit.*

In addition to sentencing for contempt, a superior court of record has unlimited powers of imposing fines. S14(4A)[9] of the Contempt of Court Act 1981 makes clear that the County Court is a superior court of record for this purpose only (but note that the County Court is an inferior court of record other than for this purpose).

The family court appears to have its jurisdiction limited because the family court gets its jurisdiction from section of the Matrimonial and Family Proceedings Act 1984[10] . The effect being that the family court

---

[9] (4A) For the purposes of the preceding provisions of this section the county court shall be treated as a superior court and not as an inferior court.

9. 31E Family court has High Court and county court powers

(1) In any proceedings in the family court, the court may make any order—

(a) **which could be made by the High Court if the proceedings were in the High Court, or**

(b) which could be made by the county court if the proceedings were in the county court.

(2) In its application to a power of the High Court to issue a writ directed to an enforcement officer, subsection (1)(a) gives the family court power to issue a warrant, directed to an officer of the family court, containing provision corresponding to any that might be contained in the writ.

(3) Subsection (1) is subject to section 38(3) of the County Courts Act 1984.

can make any orders which could be made if the made in the High Court or County Court. Note that in the family court the fine imposable appears to be a maximum of £2500, unless made by a High Court Judge.

It is essential to deal fully and appropriately with the penalty to be imposed (the sentence). This might be on a different occasion to the finding of contempt hearing. The Defendant must be given a proper opportunity to address the court in respect of the penalty/sentence.

The powers to suspend a sentence exist, albeit on even wider terms than available in the criminal courts.

Giving a discount for an admission (a 'plea of guilty') is appropriate and must be considered. Indeed, it will encourage alleged contemnors to act more appropriately if they have committed a breach to more readily admit their fault if they know that the court will impose a lesser sentence by providing a discount for an admission of a breach of an order or undertaking.

Once imprisoned by an order of committal, a contemnor will only serve on half of the sentence imposed.

There is no community penalty option available as there is in the Crown Court.

---

(4) Subsection (1) is without prejudice to, and not limited by, any other powers of the family court.

(5) The Lord Chancellor may by regulations make provision, about or in connection with the effect or execution of warrants issued by the family court for enforcing any order or judgment enforceable by the court, that corresponds to any provision applying in relation to the effect or execution of writs issued by the High Court, or warrants issued by the county court, for the purpose of enforcing any order or judgment enforceable by that court.

CHAPTER TEN

APPEALS

It is clear that a person against whom an order of committal to prison is made or against whom a suspended sentence is imposed is entitled as of right to appeal. That person does not require permission to appeal. It is essential to inform the contemnor of this right and so it is vital that care is taken to ensure that the proceedings were both procedurally fair and that the correct decision was reached.

The decision in **Liverpool v Zafar** [2019] EWCA Civ 392, [2019] 1 WLR 3833 referred to above at chapter nine respect of appeals helpfully sets out how the court will assess an appeal.

There is some limited debate as to whether a contemnor requires permission to appeal though if they have not been the subject of an actual or suspended order for of committal to prison. For example, if the contemnor has 'only' been fined for their contempt.

It is suggested by some that the difference arises by virtue of CPR Part 52.3(1)(a)(i)[11] and CPR Part 81.8(7).

There is also the Access to Justice Act 1960 ("AJA 1960") provides as follows:

> *"13 Appeal in cases of contempt of court.*

---

[11] CPR Part 52.3.1(a)(i) (1) An appellant or respondent requires permission to appeal—

> (a) where the appeal is from a decision of a judge in the County Court or the High Court, or to the Court of Appeal from a decision of a judge in the family court, except where the appeal is against:

(i) a committal order

> *(1) Subject to the provisions of this section, an appeal shall lie under this section from any order or decision of a court in the exercise of jurisdiction to punish for contempt of court (including criminal contempt); and in relation to any such order or decision the provisions of this section shall have effect in substitution for any other enactment relating to appeals in civil or criminal proceedings.*
>
> *(2) An appeal under this section shall lie in any case at the instance of the defendant and, in the case of an application for committal or attachment, at the instance of the applicant; and the appeal shall lie—*
>
> ...
>
> *(b) from an order or decision of the county court or any other inferior court from which appeals generally lie to the Court of Appeal, and from an order or decision (other than a decision on an appeal under this section) of a single judge of the High Court, or of any court having the powers of the High Court or of a judge of that court, to the Court of Appeal;*
>
> ...
>
> *(3) The court to which an appeal is brought under this section may reverse or vary the order or decision of the court below, and make such other order as may be just; and without prejudice to the inherent powers of any court referred to in subsection (2) of this section...."*
>
> *43. The AJA 1960 should be read alongside CPR 52.21 (Hearing of Appeals)..."*

In my view it would appear that until the Court of Appeal deals with such a point brought before it, the safer and fairer course is to inform contemnors that they have a right of appeal to the appeal court and that permission to appeal is not required. Even when the penalty imposed for the finding of contempt does not result in an actual or suspended order of committal to prison.

CHECKLIST

It is easy to get tangled in the main proceedings and for errors to be made in respect of the actual contempt proceedings.

This checklist may provide a useful aid memoire and tick box to ensure that as many steps as possible are remembered by both the judge and the advocates[12].

1. The Judge and the Advocates are to be robed.
2. The hearing shall be in open court.
3. The Defendant must be aged 18 or over.
4. The Defendant must not lack capacity.
5. The Defendant must be told they have the right to silence and that they cannot be compelled to give evidence. The Defendant is to be reminded of the right against self-incrimination.
6. The Defendant is entitled to be legally represented and to non-means-tested Legal Aid. See Chapter 4.
7. Has the Defendant had sufficient time to prepare?
8. Is permission required by the Claimant to bring the contempt proceedings? See Chapters 7 and 8.
9. Generally, the contempt application must be personally served on the Defendant.
10. Was there a penal notice on the order or undertakings which are now being used as the springboard for these contempt

[12] There will be some exceptional cases in which not all will apply, for example, there might be exceptional reasons why the proceedings will be unrobed and not in open court. However, the court and parties must be aware of the essential rules and procedure and will need to explain why the essential rules and procedure was not followed in any particular case.

proceedings? Is there a proper warning endorsed on the face of that order or undertaking in respect of committal?

11. Was the original court order or the undertakings clear as to what the Defendant must or must not do with a penal notice attached?

12. Was there personal service of the order or undertaking?

13. Has the committal application set out the alleged breaches of the order or undertakings in a clear and correct manner?

14. Does the Claimant's evidence set out and properly identify what the alleged breaches are?

15. At the hearing, make appropriate adjustments to deal with the Defendant's participation and to ensure that there is a fair hearing such as with the use of interpreters if required and to proceed with the hearing at the Defendant's pace. Use appropriate measures to assist all of the parties and witnesses to achieve a fair outcome, such as special measures for the parties or witnesses when giving their evidence. Use the Equal Treatment Bench Book.

16. The burden of proof is on the person bringing the contempt proceedings.

17. The standard of proof is the criminal standard whereby the allegations must be proved beyond reasonable doubt. Namely, the court must be satisfied so that it is sure that there has been a breach of the order or undertakings.

18. The Court should pause at the end of the hearing and consider if the evidence meets the criminal standard for each of the separate allegations. The order needs to make clear what the findings are that establish the contempt of court.

19. If the Court decides that one or more of the allegations are proved to the required standard of proof, then it should adjourn before imposing its penalty.

20. If the contemnor had failed to attend the hearing, then issue a warrant for their arrest to bring them before the court.

21. The Court should not impose its penalty without first hearing from the contemnor or from their advocate.

22. The maximum imprisonment by an order of committal is two years for each breach. Ensure that mitigation is heard. Suspended orders of committal to prison can made. There are also other non-custodial options available to the court, but not community penalties. See Chapter 9.

23. Inform the contemnor of their right to appeal and that permission to appeal is not required. See Chapter 10.

24. The Court is to complete the court forms for contempt and for the publication of the judgment setting out the reasons for its decision

MORE BOOKS BY LAW BRIEF PUBLISHING

'Covid-19, Homeworking and the Law – The Essential Guide to Employment and GDPR Issues' by Forbes Solicitors

'Covid-19, Force Majeure and Frustration of Contracts – The Essential Guide' by Keith Markham

'Covid-19 and Criminal Law – The Essential Guide' by Ramya Nagesh

'Covid-19 and Family Law in England and Wales – The Essential Guide' by Safda Mahmood

'A Practical Guide to the Law of Unlawful Eviction and Harassment – 2nd Edition' by Stephanie Lovegrove

'Covid-19, Residential Property, Equity Release and Enfranchisement – The Essential Guide' by Paul Sams and Louise Uphill

'Covid-19, Brexit and the Law of Commercial Leases – The Essential Guide' by Mark Shelton

'A Practical Guide to Costs in Personal Injury Claims – 2nd Edition' by Matthew Hoe

'A Practical Guide to the General Data Protection Regulation (GDPR) – 2nd Edition' by Keith Markham

'Ellis on Credit Hire – Sixth Edition' by Aidan Ellis & Tim Kevan

'A Practical Guide to Working with Litigants in Person and McKenzie Friends in Family Cases' by Stuart Barlow

'Protecting Unregistered Brands: A Practical Guide to the Law of Passing Off' by Lorna Brazell

'A Practical Guide to Secondary Liability and Joint Enterprise Post-Jogee' by Joanne Cecil & James Mehigan

'A Practical Guide to the Pre-Action RTA Claims Protocol for Personal Injury Lawyers' by Antonia Ford

'A Practical Guide to Neighbour Disputes and the Law' by Alexander Walsh

'A Practical Guide to Forfeiture of Leases' by Mark Shelton

'A Practical Guide to Coercive Control for Legal Practitioners and Victims' by Rachel Horman

'A Practical Guide to Rights Over Airspace and Subsoil' by Daniel Gatty

'Tackling Disclosure in the Criminal Courts – A Practitioner's Guide' by Narita Bahra QC & Don Ramble

'A Practical Guide to the Law of Driverless Cars – Second Edition' by Alex Glassbrook, Emma Northey & Scarlett Milligan

'A Practical Guide to TOLATA Claims' by Greg Williams

'Artificial Intelligence – The Practical Legal Issues' by John Buyers

'A Practical Guide to the Law of Prescription in Scotland' by Andrew Foyle

'A Practical Guide to the Construction and Rectification of Wills and Trust Instruments' by Edward Hewitt

'A Practical Guide to the Law of Bullying and Harassment in the Workplace' by Philip Hyland

'How to Be a Freelance Solicitor: A Practical Guide to the SRA-Regulated Freelance Solicitor Model' by Paul Bennett

'A Practical Guide to Prison Injury Claims' by Malcolm Johnson

'A Practical Guide to the Small Claims Track' by Dominic Bright

'A Practical Guide to Advising Clients at the Police Station' by Colin Stephen McKeown-Beaumont

'A Practical Guide to Antisocial Behaviour Injunctions' by Iain Wightwick

'Practical Mediation: A Guide for Mediators, Advocates, Advisers, Lawyers, and Students in Civil, Commercial, Business, Property, Workplace, and Employment Cases' by Jonathan Dingle with John Sephton

'The Mini-Pupillage Workbook' by David Boyle

'A Practical Guide to Crofting Law' by Brian Inkster

'A Practical Guide to Spousal Maintenance' by Liz Cowell

'A Practical Guide to the Law of Domain Names and Cybersquatting' by Andrew Clemson

'A Practical Guide to the Law of Gender Pay Gap Reporting' by Harini Iyengar

'A Practical Guide to the Rights of Grandparents in Children Proceedings' by Stuart Barlow
'NHS Whistleblowing and the Law' by Joseph England
'Employment Law and the Gig Economy' by Nigel Mackay & Annie Powell
'A Practical Guide to Noise Induced Hearing Loss (NIHL) Claims' by Andrew Mckie, Ian Skeate, Gareth McAloon
'An Introduction to Beauty Negligence Claims – A Practical Guide for the Personal Injury Practitioner' by Greg Almond
'Intercompany Agreements for Transfer Pricing Compliance' by Paul Sutton
'Zen and the Art of Mediation' by Martin Plowman
'A Practical Guide to the SRA Principles, Individual and Law Firm Codes of Conduct 2019 – What Every Law Firm Needs to Know' by Paul Bennett
'A Practical Guide to Adoption for Family Lawyers' by Graham Pegg
'A Practical Guide to Industrial Disease Claims' by Andrew Mckie & Ian Skeate
'A Practical Guide to Redundancy' by Philip Hyland
'A Practical Guide to Vicarious Liability' by Mariel Irvine
'A Practical Guide to Applications for Landlord's Consent and Variation of Leases' by Mark Shelton
'A Practical Guide to Relief from Sanctions Post-Mitchell and Denton' by Peter Causton
'A Practical Guide to Equity Release for Advisors' by Paul Sams
'A Practical Guide to the Law Relating to Food' by Ian Thomas
'A Practical Guide to Financial Services Claims' by Chris Hegarty
'The Law of Houses in Multiple Occupation: A Practical Guide to HMO Proceedings' by Julian Hunt
'A Practical Guide to Unlawful Eviction and Harassment' by Stephanie Lovegrove
'Occupiers, Highways and Defective Premises Claims: A Practical Guide Post-Jackson – 2nd Edition' by Andrew Mckie

'A Practical Guide to Financial Ombudsman Service Claims' by Adam Temple & Robert Scrivenor
'A Practical Guide to Advising Schools on Employment Law' by Jonathan Holden
'A Practical Guide to Running Housing Disrepair and Cavity Wall Claims: 2nd Edition' by Andrew Mckie & Ian Skeate
'A Practical Guide to Holiday Sickness Claims – 2nd Edition' by Andrew Mckie & Ian Skeate
'Arguments and Tactics for Personal Injury and Clinical Negligence Claims' by Dorian Williams
'A Practical Guide to Drone Law' by Rufus Ballaster, Andrew Firman, Eleanor Clot
'A Practical Guide to Compliance for Personal Injury Firms Working With Claims Management Companies' by Paul Bennett
'A Practical Guide to Dog Law for Owners and Others' by Andrea Pitt
'RTA Allegations of Fraud in a Post-Jackson Era: The Handbook – 2nd Edition' by Andrew Mckie
'RTA Personal Injury Claims: A Practical Guide Post-Jackson' by Andrew Mckie
'On Experts: CPR35 for Lawyers and Experts' by David Boyle
'An Introduction to Personal Injury Law' by David Boyle
'A Practical Guide to Subtle Brain Injury Claims' by Pankaj Madan

These books and more are available to order online direct from the publisher at www.lawbriefpublishing.com, where you can also read free sample chapters. For any queries, contact us on 0844 587 2383 or mail@lawbriefpublishing.com.

Our books are also usually in stock at www.amazon.co.uk with free next day delivery for Prime members, and at good legal bookshops such as Wildy & Sons.

We are regularly launching new books in our series of practical day-to-day practitioners' guides. Visit our website and join our free newsletter to be kept informed and to receive special offers, free chapters, etc.

You can also follow us on Twitter at www.twitter.com/lawbriefpub.

www.ingramcontent.com/pod-product-compliance
Lightning Source LLC
LaVergne TN
LVHW022106200926
848481LV00003B/1074